THE PRINCE AND THE PENCIL PUSHER

ROYAL POWERS BOOK 7

KENZIE BLADES

Dear Kat,

Thank you for visiting me in Edinburgh!

— Kenzie

LUXE PRESS

Dear Kat,

Thank you for visiting me in Edinburgh!

— Tomas

PART I

THE MINISTRY OF POWERS

CHAPTER ONE

Xabier

"How soon can you arrive?" Fesik did not wait for my answer. "I'm afraid I'm desperate for your talents. The fruit is too small and far too cool on the vine."

"Which varietal?" I quizzed. Understanding the severity of the issue meant knowing which grape we were dealing with.

"The Syrah," he replied.

Syrah was a hearty grape, but it couldn't hold up to what was happening in the north. That is, the northern part of the south. The vineyards we were speaking of were in South Abarra, my home country and the only Abarra worth belonging to. Fesik was in Palamos, where the best grapes were grown, and I was stuck at work in Dulibre, the city on the border. Like Abarra itself, Dulibre was split into north and south.

"At this rate, they won't come close to ripening by harvestide," Fesik continued. My friend was excitable on a good day and I could not blame his worry now. Winemaking was a delicate art and the season had been cool. Every day that passed without warm air and sun bleakened the crop's prospects. But grapes sometimes had plans of their own.

"Brix?" I demanded, evening out my breath. Both of us panicking wouldn't do. Before I would allow myself an outburst, it was incumbent upon me to gather the facts.

Brix was a special measure that gauged the sugar content of wine grapes. It allowed winemakers to understand their ripeness with precision before the fruit in question was ever harvested. It wasn't an exaggeration to call myself the country's foremost expert. Brix was kind of my thing.

"Nineteen." Fesik sounded miserable as he spit out the number that shot a stab of panic up the side of my neck. Desirable levels were between twenty-three and twenty-six. Numbers like these so close to the harvest was a terrible sign. It made me want to abandon the confines of my posh office that had only ever felt like a cage, and trade them for freezing vineyards and a task that would render me helpful. Contrary to infuriatingly popular belief, I was of no use here.

"pH levels?" I asked with a dreadful feeling.

"Out of range," Fesik reported. "Titratable acidity as well. With all due respect, Your Grace, if we don't get a handle on this, we're fucked."

Fesik rarely showed me all due respect, which was exactly what I liked about him. We had to be equals in order to make the wine we did. All true partnerships thrived on an honest exchange of ideas.

What brought us together was wanting the same thing: to make the finest, most envied wine in all of Abarra. We wanted our wine to win the prestigious Abarra Wine Prize—again. We wanted to maintain bragging rights and continue to best our unfriendliest of neighbors in the north. Also in it for me was awaited recognition. Who better to bask in his winemaking accolades than I, Prince Xabier Garrastazu, Duke of Brix?

Knowing so much about brix was severely undervalued in

my day job, a circumstance that I was working to change. If I couldn't make my day job care about wine making, then I would just have to find a new one. In the meantime, working at my true calling would have to remain unofficial. Strictly speaking, what I did for Fesik was moonlighting.

"I'll come as soon as I can," I vowed, my voice more bitter than apologetic. Fesik knew the strength of my tethers. Even on a Friday evening—especially so—duty called. My constraints made me undesirable. Apart from my facility with the libation, I would not have been any partner's first choice.

It was my power that served as an incentive for Fesik to tolerate me—my uncanny and mysterious ability to ripen grape clusters to my liking. By simply bestowing my energy onto the fruit, I could infuse it with the correct levels of sugar. I could change the interior makeup of the grapes—turn them into what they wanted to be—and make them ready for picking just in time.

"One more frost and they'll be beyond repair." Fesik's voice was grim.

If I got there soon, I could prevent such a fate. But in order to do that, I had to make the three-hour journey from South Dulibre to Palamos.

"I'll arrange for transport by evening." I lowered my voice to speak the promise. "It'll be midnight by the time I make it, but early enough to ward off frost."

Fesik's voice became chilly. "You know the grapes don't like to be meddled with when they're already too cold. Just this once, can't you make an exception and travel by royal plane?"

"Fesik..." I warned. "You know very well that such a mode of transport is reserved for important matters of state."

I could practically hear him lift his chin. "Winning the Abarra Wine Prize qualifies as such."

"You know very well that I cannot simply summon the plane, and you know even better why my activities in the vineyards must remain a secret. I have been forbidden by the Queen."

Admitting the truth out loud always made me queasy. Technically speaking, there had been an "if." I was forbidden from wine making *if* doing so would compromise my duties at the Ministry of Powers.

On the one hand, I had precious few duties because I didn't take my post very seriously. On the other hand, I needed to maintain the appearance of performing said duties, being available, and adding value in some way. I was the highest-ranking official in the agency: the Minister of Powers himself.

"No good will come from prolonging the lie, Xabier. You said it yourself last season. This year will be the year that you tell the Queen."

My eyes darted around my office, as if I were the one speaking and the walls were the ears of royal spies. They swept over my leftmost monitor, which displayed the security feed. I was relieved to see Eusebio, my assistant, engrossed in a book. The monitor showed two frames; the other was the approach from the grand hallway—empty—in the frame on the right.

"I did say that, didn't I?" My reply was absent in its paranoia.

For the moment, praise for our wine was showered solely upon Fesik. It bothered him to take all the glory. My only mark was *Ichor*, the name I had bestowed upon our prizewinning blend. In Greek mythology, it meant an ethereal fluid thought to be the blood of the gods. In the irony of all ironies, the labor of love which took my attentions away from my very-important-slash-boring day job was adored by my aunt, the Queen, Maialen.

"Before midnight," I repeated then hung up the phone, figuring I'd better go from talking to doing. Fesik's call had come in on my personal phone. In the Ministry of Powers, one had to be discreet about matters that one wanted to keep to oneself. So also must one do when one was a royal.

For the most part, I had whittled down the number of servants and guards, becoming self-sufficient enough to keep supervision at a minimum. Yet there was one who stood a chance at thwarting my plans to travel to Palamos. And he wouldn't be so easy to shake off.

"Abide your duties," he would say, coated in his own brand of sugar that skirted the rules of subordination. Zain Otxoa possessed the rare ability to deliver bizarrely respectful scoldings. He was quite tricky in that respect. He was quite tricky in other respects, as well. He was why I was loath to leave my post without covering my tracks.

I switched to my old-style intercom and watched on the monitor as Eusebio startled at my buzz. The man was grossly underutilized—fit to assist someone with a full schedule and dozens of difficult tasks. On the rare occasion I actually summoned him, he would nearly jump out of his skin, too eager to oblige.

"Eusebio. I need a car for the evening, please."

"Immediately, Your Grace?" He straightened in his seat, tossing the thick tome he had been reading onto the desk. I might have liked him better had he read something serious like Dostoyevsky, or something trashy, like gossip rags. But he only ever read the most boring book on earth: *The Policies and Procedures Manual of the Ministry of Powers*.

"I'll take a pickup in fifteen minutes. Around the back, please."

"Yes, Your Grace." I watched Eusebio write down the simple instruction. "Shall I specify a destination?"

"I'll give it to the driver when he arrives." My voice was calm. If I gave a nothing out-of-the-ordinary vibe, there would be nothing for Eusebio to suspect.

"And your proxy, Your Grace?"

I was not permitted to go off duty without one, though the Day and Night Deputy Ministers were my second and third in command, respectively. Between the three of us, we worked a twenty-four-hour shift. As the Minister, I had the "honor" of taking the shifts when the most critical incidents occurred. Though I resented it, it *was* a great honor—a high office befitting a high royal, assuming responsibility for the most extraordinary aspect of our world. In Abarra, royals had superpowers.

"Super" may have been too strong a word for some of the abilities the gods had bestowed upon the ruling class. Nonetheless, those who possessed such powers were called "supos." There was nothing to joke about when it came to superpowers run amok. Royals were required to register their powers. The Ministry was intended to provide guidance, education and, frankly, intimidation to discourage their misuse.

"Please ask Duke Oleander to be on call."

"Certainly, my lord."

It was my duty to know about incidents and to help bring said incidents to resolution. Since only royals could possess these powers, it was thought (quite erroneously) that abuses were rare. That the royal family, as custodians of the public trust, acted responsibly. Little did Abarra know how far the Ministry had to go to diffuse dangerous situations. Seeing what came in on most Friday and Saturday nights was like watching an episode of *Royals Gone Wild*.

"And Eusebio? I see no need to trouble Mr. Otxoa with information about my whereabouts. Should he drop by, simply let him know that I placed matters in Duke Oleander's capable hands."

Apart from my Deputy Ministers, he was my highest lieutenant, and the man hellbent on insisting that I have absolutely no fun.

"You can let him know yourself, Your Grace. Mr. Otxoa just entered the hall."

My eyes flew to the right half of the monitor display. As surely as Eusebio had indicated, Zain Otxoa was beating a path to my door. His timing was so uncanny, it was as if he knew.

CHAPTER TWO

Zain

Not so fast.

My heels clicked in rapid succession as I walked down the centerline of the grand executive hall. It was far afield of the offices on the lower floors. It took minutes to get all the way up there, which was why I'd needed to make haste. When left unattended on nights when he would rather have been any place but at his post, the Prince had a tendency to disappear.

The floor in the hall was made of marble and its design was quite ornate—a wide, white border off to each side, with an elaborate design forming a runway down the middle. It wasn't a pattern but a work of art, its geometric pieces reminiscent of stained glass. It gave the sense of walking on a rug made of stone.

Hues from garnet, to ruby, to tawny, to rose made up elements of a palette that swirled and faded to ambers and golds. They complemented magnificent oil paintings of Abarran countryside that lined the grand corridor's high walls. Spaced-out sitting benches rendered the space worthy of entertaining. Yet, he kept it to himself, and spent most of his time alone.

The downstairs offices were another story. They were filled with six-by-six-foot cubicles configured en masse for the Ministry's rank and file. Enclosed offices here and there were reserved for mid-level managers: MLMs, as we liked to call them. I inhabited one of the better of these offices—a space in the corner on a higher floor with a not-bad view—though an MLM I was not.

Ostensibly, I was the Head of Internal Affairs, which was exactly the Queen's intention—a gross understatement considering my deep involvement with the covert side. Not making that last fact public was by design. My list of responsibilities was too long to name—too long for me to remember most days. Yet, the highest of my duties was to babysit *him*.

He was Prince Xabier Garrastazu, third in line to the South Abarran throne, son of Prince Frantzisco, nephew to the Queen, and Duke of Brix. He was also the Minister of Powers—the highest-ranking official at this agency and, despite my charge to keep him from making too big a mess out of things, he was technically my boss.

"Is he in?" I asked Eusebio, more for his benefit than mine. I knew the Prince's comings and goings. I had eyes on him at all times. I tried not to roll my eyes as Eusebio made a production of picking up the phone to announce my arrival. The Prince enjoyed forcing me to wait to be let in.

Good.

The more ridiculously childish and infuriatingly vain Prince Xabier, Duke of Brix, chose to be wherever I was concerned, the easier it was to ignore his ridiculous appeal.

"Your Grace." As usual, I greeted his back, the part of him that always seemed to face me when I walked into his suite. Even from behind, the man was magnificent. Broad shoulders filled out a perfectly tailored button-down made of fine fabric and subtle herringbone design. Today's shirt—white, if you weren't paying attention—was the faintest of lilac. He was the epitome of a dashing prince.

To be clear, I *was* paying attention, not only to the way its snug fit showed the definition in his shoulders—to the place where the fabric stopped and his rolled-up sleeves gave way to skin. For all the hard work he didn't do, there needn't have been any rolling up of sleeves. In my most outlandish of theories, he did it to torment me.

"Mr. Otxoa," the Prince greeted blithely, not turning toward me just yet. He stood on a rug in the sitting area with his gaze remained fixed on the fire and his face in profile. His office was a projection of the man himself—pleasantly fragrant, clean to a fault and dripping with style. Tufted wingback chairs with ottomans flanked a matching Chesterfield, all three in a dark teal. Fire glow warmed his features, casting appeal on the planes of his face, flattering the smooth line of his nose and cutting shadows from his diamond jaw.

I stopped at the edge of the rug next to the drink trolley that carried only wine. Its twin at the other end of the Chesterfield was all crystal decanters and spirits. When he turned, I was meant to bow out of deference. This was always the most difficult moment—the one when he first cast his gaze upon me. I faltered at the devastating beauty of his eyes.

"And what have you for me tonight? More documents to sign, no doubt. More supos with powers run rampant?"

He made no secret of the fact that my presence vexed him. Unencumbered by the burden of common birth, the Prince was under no obligation to feign politesse. Logic dictated that his resentment stemmed from me holding him to task. Instinct told me that the sport he made of pushing my buttons was something more.

The Prince finally cast his sapphire gaze upon me and I did bow then, thankful that the deep hue of my skin made it easy to hide my flush. Blood that he could not see rushed to my cheeks and prickled my nose and burned the tops of my ears. If he resented me, I, too, resented him. Training the Prince was not supposed to be so difficult as this.

He motioned toward the folder in my hand, knowing what papers it contained, impatient to sign off and have me gone.

"It would be best if we could discuss them, Your Grace. To understand each one, end-to-end."

"Yet, you understand the crimes, Mr. Otxoa, do you not?" He took the folder from my hand and began to leaf through.

"Yes, Your Grace, I do."

"And you *are* fit to bring them to resolution...?" His entire line of questioning was a trap. Baiting me in such a manner would be the Prince's latest gambit to get me out.

It wouldn't be the first time he had schemed to cast doubt upon my capabilities. He'd harped on a mass impregnation at the South Abarra Kennel Club Dog Show that had happened on my watch, as if I—and not Count Cesar, the Cupid of Canines—had been the cause of the problem. The man wanted me gone from the Ministry. Expecting things of him made his life more difficult. He'd attempted to orchestrate my termination at least thrice.

"I do worry, Your Grace, of what might occur if I were away from my post. I would want to ensure that you were fully prepared."

"Do you mean to imply that I am unprepared, Mr. Otxoa?" He arched an eyebrow.

His eyes did something spectacular when he was in a wicked mood. They narrowed and darkened and focused in bold confrontation. It was wrong of me to bait him when I knew well how to calm the waters. But I, too, had grown addicted to the thrill.

"Of course not, Your Grace." I bowed. "I meant only to suggest that matters of such import to national security should only be left to hands as capable as yours. And that you, as the Minister, should be apprised of all serious matters. Wet Willie struck again just an hour ago."

The tension in the Prince's eyes softened and the corner of his mouth crooked upward. The spectacular thing that his face did when he smiled was something else entirely.

"Is that so?" His eyes dropped to the tablet in my hand. The folder held the actual paperwork that needed his signature, but the tablet held the digital files.

"What's old Willie been up to?" the Prince asked with a widening smile.

Duke Guillermo of Mutriku had the power to cause spontaneous floods. It came in handy during the occasional drought. That was one reason why the Ministry had strived to keep things with Guillermo—Willie, for short—on good terms. Easier said than done given his penchant for showmanship.

"He got himself cast as Moses in a production of *Exodus*." I tapped around on my device. "The scene about parting the Red Sea turned out to be a real show-stopper. It created a tidal wave that submerged the crowd. The water rose so high, most of the orchestra pit wound up swimming to safety on the balcony. Nobody was killed, thank the gods."

I took a step closer and handed the Prince the device. As he leafed through the photos, I knew what he would see: the sour faces of otherwise well-dressed victims who looked no better than sewer rats with blankets; the sodden interior of The Royal Theater with all but the bolted down chairs thrown askew; a photo of Guillermo, still in his costume of opulent robes and dry as a bone.

Since only royals had powers, they were not treated as common criminals when they were detained. Rather, they were chauffeured in an official Ministry limousine, served pintxos and wine, and loosened up quite a bit to soften the reprimand that was sure to come.

"Any injuries?" the Prince wanted to know.

"Minor ones," I answered. "Flotsam from the rising tide. A number of theatergoers have called for his exile. The Marquess of Tuile thinks he ought to be sent abroad on a service mission to revive dry riverbeds in countries where we wish to build diplomatic ties."

"Not a bad idea..." the Prince murmured. "The Duke is back in his manor now, I presume?"

He looked through the photos, brow furrowed. It proved I had his attention. It proved something else the Prince worked hard to conceal: that he cared.

It had occurred to me more than once that he only hated his post because he felt helpless. The Prince did not belong behind a desk. His instinct was to be out in all manner of literal and figurative fields, feeling that he could be useful. Every shred of sympathy I felt for him came from that.

If only he knew his real task...

But I was not at liberty to get into all of that. Instead, I answered his question.

"On house vacation," I confirmed. It was the polite term we used to describe the circumstance of a royal who had been escorted home and provided with a round-the-clock servant-slash-bodyguard who worked for the Ministry. When commoners were relegated to their homes, we called it by its real name: house arrest.

"At absolute least, I assume we plan to ban him from The Royal Theater? Next season's production is King Arthur. Rumor has it he's set to audition for *Lady of the Lake*."

I directed him to the recommended punitive measures that I had drafted.

"I've written in a tightening of his restrictions. He's already been banned from sporting events and concerts, public seasonal festivities, all municipal buildings and—after last year's unfortunate incident at Queen Maialen's birthday party—from the palace itself."

"Must we go to greater extremes?" The Prince had yet to scan the agreement. Instead, he looked at me.

"To keep people safe, yes."

Despite all the rules and the registries and the warnings, royals were an impossible group to control. They possessed wealth, power, ingrained entitlement, and they weren't always the smartest. Most of those with wilder tendencies fell in line and curbed their powers eventually, but not before they had pushed audaciously at the limits. The worst repeat offenders weren't the ones who couldn't control their powers—they were the ones who could control them but thought they were above being mandated to do so.

"Anything else?"

By then, the Prince had handed me back the tablet and was walking himself—and the folder full of incident resolution forms—to his desk. He began to sign them without reading them, a true test to my sanity. I could not comprehend his blind trust.

"Nothing active, but we do consider this to be a high-risk evening. We've got the alert level on Defense Condition Four."

"I'm afraid I won't be able to stay. I've been called away on business."

"What sort of business?" I asked, and remembered just in time to slip in a "Your Grace."

"My own," he replied a bit curtly.

"My apologies, Your Grace. When you said business, I assumed that you meant something related to the Ministry. I was pleased with the notion that you had a case to work. I assumed that any Friday night outing would be strictly professionally oriented, seeing as how it has been your habit to miss so much time from work."

I didn't miss the light scowl on his face, as if I had said

something terrible instead of something true. He did not always enjoy it when I chose to be blunt. But our standoffs were utterly necessary. If I did not challenge the Prince, what license he took would place the needs of the future beyond reach.

"I will return tomorrow afternoon," he continued. "If anything happens, you are to reach me personally by telephone. Are you able to follow those orders?"

I bowed once more. "Yes, Your Grace."

"Keep the place together, Mr. Otxoa."

CHAPTER THREE

Xabier
　　The journey to Palamos was a scenic drive when taken from South Dulibre, though the mountains in the distance and rolling vineyards were difficult to see in the dark. Despite the late hour, my alertness rose the deeper I drove into the country. The weather outside was cold, but I kept the window of the car cracked, enjoying the smell of the air as it changed in pungency and in freshness. Some untold essence it held rejuvenated me.

My childhood home was not far from here. These had once been my family's lands, back in the days when feudal lords had ruled. The Duchy of Palamos was still presided over by my father. Mostly symbolic now, the title would one day pass down to me.

Fesik, for his part, was a childhood friend—the slightly older son of the late winemaker, Fasad, who had run my own family's vineyards as a child. The hundred-acre vineyards where Fesik now grew our wine had been a gift from my father to Fasad for decades of extraordinary service.

"You've come just in time."

Fesik opened the door to my chauffeured car—not out of respect, but out of urgency—before the car came to a full stop. The limousine—of the armored variety with both driver and bodyguard in the front seat—had slowed the deeper we'd gotten into the vineyard.

"Which lots are the worst?" He shuffled me directly into a waiting golf cart, jumped inside himself and put his foot on the gas. A quick lurch forward had me gripping the pole that connected the roof and the dash.

"The ones on the western border," he hollered loudly over the sound of the engine and the rushing air. The small vehicle flew through the night.

As we reached the correct area, one that I knew even in the dark, Fesik slowed the cart and turned off the headlights, knowing well our routine.

"Cut the engine," I instructed based on an instinct I had never been able to explain. I always knew when I reached where I needed to be. It was half of the reason why some part of me actually enjoyed heading off a good frost. Inside my body, my power felt like heat.

Already, it burned in my chest, for now slightly vague yet still brimming with anticipation. It would grow more intense, but not much. The real heat liked to creep up my forearms and stretch to my fingers. It wasn't a burning sort of heat; it was more like a restorative warmth that gathered in my palms and felt like life itself.

"These," I proclaimed. Now it was my turn to hop out of the vehicle before it had even stopped. I stalked directly between the rows in the vineyard. The one to my left was planted with Garnacha—a fact I could tell as much by sense as by memory. They would need help this night, too. For now, I would begin with the Syrah.

It always started with a cluster. Instinct guided me to which one. I left it on the vine but held it in my cupped hands. I don't know what others saw in such moments but, in my own mind's eye, the object of my focus was cast in a golden glow, as if a single ray of sunlight shone through the darkness. In that moment, I gave them warmth. Somehow, I could taste juice in my mouth as I worked my magic and see it as the glow turned from golden to purple. I knew exactly how far I had to go, to get it to the right flavor. I could tell when I had to stop.

Conscious of Fesik behind me, paces away to give me space, I dropped one hand from the cluster and beckoned him over. The warmth was concentrated to my hands but my whole body was alive. It was euphoric, drug-like, finer than the feeling of smoking opium and not without its own brand of withdrawal. When I did not do this, and often, I missed it.

That part of it was tragic to the extent that wine grapes did not need constant warming throughout the year. Now, we were nearing the end of the season. If the weather did as expected, this would be my last time.

Fesik flipped open the hood of his refractometer and plucked off a grape from the cluster that still rested in one hand. With my other hand, I took a grape as well. Fesik squeezed the juice of his grape between his fingers, hard, getting every drop onto the sensor of the small machine that measured brix and acidity and pH. At the very same moment, I slipped the fruit into my own mouth. I was already smiling—quite ridiculously, I imagined. Chewing the tiny sphere of perfection only made me smile harder.

"Yes." Fesik's voice broke me from my euphoria. I reopened my eyes against the night. He blinked quickly against tears. My frozen breath—now sweet with juice—were tiny clouds that seemed to glow a purple hue.

I nodded back, then raised my hands, crossing upturned palms above my head. In my mind's eye I held every Syrah cluster in the vineyard, all at once in my warmed hands. I fed the golden glow in my palm, turning every Syrah grape in the vineyard until the energy in my hands grew purple. I swooned when it was all done.

∼

BY THE TIME I finished with the last of the Tempranillo clusters, dawn was breaking over the vineyards. The temperature had stayed above the frost point all night, but only just. Nights like this were capped by warm, wine-soaked breakfasts served reluctantly by Fesik's groggy wife, Odelia. She had awakened in the middle of the night to prepare a feast not only for us, but for my chauffeur and guard too.

"Your abilities ... they are changing," Fesik complemented, looking as energized as I felt despite the late hour. Under the house light, I could clearly see his face. He could not have been more my opposite. I was tall and athletic with dark ginger hair and blue eyes. He was shorter in stature, broader in the shoulders and burlier overall, all sable, curly hair and deep brown eyes.

"Changing how?" I thought twice about picking up a fourth arraultza. Odelia was quite a good cook, which said a lot, considering my access to fineries all around.

"This time it was unmistakable. You're not just altering the sugar content. You're changing the pH."

"Adding sugar always lowers pH."

"By predictable levels," Fesik agreed. "Sometimes increasing the sugar lowers it too much. Out there just now...it didn't lower as much as it should have." He leaned in. "You're becoming more powerful, Xabi. If this is how it can be, it means our streak has just begun."

I picked up the arraultza, too thrilled by the notion to speak, and chewed thoughtfully around crostini and chorizo and egg. What made Odelia's arraultza great was the way she caramelized the onion.

"Have you not felt it? Even I could feel it out there last night. Your power is getting stronger."

Fesik set down his own wine and looked behind himself in paranoia. Odelia had retreated, and my guard and chauffeur laughed at the other and of the table.

"You know how I loathe to stroke that enormous ego. The universe has given you more than your own fair share of gifts. But you, friend, are the wine god's greatest gift to mankind."

He motioned to a statue of Bacchus, one that had been displayed in my own home when I was a child—yet another gift from my father to his. There was something I had always admired about this representation. Bacchus was smiling, enraptured and gazing adoringly at the cup in his hand. His head was adorned with a crown of grapes.

I thought of Fesik's question. Had I felt anything different? It was becoming harder to tell. I had chalked up the heightened gratification from using my power to being so pent up. I felt petulant even to think it, but it didn't change the truth: these two years at the Ministry had been the longest and the most trying two years of my life.

"Perhaps it's better to use it less frequently," I mused, not liking this idea one iota, but voicing it nonetheless. I would continue to limit myself in this way if it made for better wine. I had been with Fesik in the vineyards at least twice weekly before Queen Maialen had asked me to serve as minister.

"Can you do nothing to change the Queen's mind?"

Fesik knew of my woes. Now that the moment of panic had passed and the grapes were saved, he was more even-headed. All year, both of us had plotted ways to get me back where I belonged. On one hand, I wanted the duty of Minister position. The role was of great importance and some part of me felt a call to lead. Only, it turned out that I was terrible at the job.

I was a man who did not like to lose. Things I couldn't master gave me anxiety. Some days, I didn't know what I wanted more—for Queen Maialen to relieve me of my duties because I was incompetent, or for her to release me back to my true calling: being here in these vineyards, making wine.

"The Queen has spies everywhere. She must have an inkling that I am not suited to the Ministry."

"Anything is an improvement over Duke Grimaud." Fesik threw me a knowing look. The former minister's reputation couldn't have been worse.

"Yes," I conceded. "By comparison, I do seem quite competent. Though, I am reminded every day that such an assessment would be false."

Fesik chuckled, his good spirits indelible owing to me having saved the wine. "The pencil pusher?" he asked. Fesik was not skilled at remembering people by name. He *was* skilled at knowing who was who based on what they did. I had complained often enough—and specifically enough—about Zain Otxoa that Fesik had given him a name.

"He's become more tolerable," I admitted. "But he still likes to hold me to task. He's all policies and procedures."

"That's not your style," Fesik murmured under his breath before piping up. "And you're the boss. Why not have him fired?"

"I tried to have him reassigned," I admitted with a chuckle of my own. "But he's been surprisingly resilient."

That was one word to describe Zain Otxoa. Every other word that came to mind was too revealing to speak out loud. Zain was excellent. Unflappable. Gorgeous, with skin the color of cedar and hazel eyes. He gave as good as he got and fuck if that didn't turn me on. I could count on one hand the people who had been quick to garner my respect. None of them had a tailor as skilled—or bone structure as flawless—as him.

It nettled me that he was also the one person who knew how unworthy I was of my post. It had always made me uncomfortable—not the sheer notion of being judged, for to be a public figure was to be judged every day. But few others had ever made me feel so inadequate. Even more so than I, the man loathed mediocrity. He was admirable. And I was a disappointment.

"He could be an ally..." Fesik suggested. "Get him to agree you're the wrong man for the job. Get him to back another horse. He must adore old Ollie."

I thought of my cousin, the Deputy Minister of Powers, technically, my second in command. Why hadn't I thought of finding my own replacement?

"He's too by-the-book for something like that," I mused. "Even toward a plan that would likely serve his interests."

Zain's life would be markedly less infuriating were I simply gone. Less entertaining as well, I surmised. I tried to do at least that. A bit of wicked humor bettered many a hopeless situation. Though, for me, seeing him each day had become sweet torture.

"Speak to Ollie, then." Fesik continued to think aloud. "For a man in his position, replacing you could be a big win."

"Grooming Duke Oleander..." I repeated aloud, liking the idea better with each passing second. It wasn't a bad plan.

CHAPTER FOUR

Zain

"This is not a good plan."

It was Tuesday afternoon and we huddled at the Prince's desk. It was so large and deep that poring over the same paperwork at the same time required being seated on the same side. I perched on one of the guest chairs, my right shoulder a foot away from his left, at the edge of my seat. My reaction was utter horror as I scanned his proposed plan for Serafina Calavia, the squirrel-taming Duchess of Calavera.

"Let the punishment fit the crime," the Prince argued in calm indignation, a tone that he had used with me before—one that pushed my buttons, as did this constant repetition of his rationale. Midweek, when daily incidents were at their lowest, we spent half days in his office working on long-term remediation plans.

Royals with a series of offenses had to be put on plans. It was ultimately the Prince's decision to determine actions. I was meant to lend consultation to ensure that plans conformed to the rules.

"She assembled a mob of fifty-seven squirrels," I practically shouted, "and commanded them to storm Lady Helene's yard. There were barking complaints for a mile radius."

"Come, now ... do squirrels really bark?" The Prince picked up the folder with the original incident report. "This makes it sound more like a cacophony of squeaks."

I ignored his quibbling and went on. "You think that a woman who got revenge on a poor old lady and her rooster by sending fifty-seven squirrels deserves a proportional response?"

On the date in question, the Duchess Serafina, who could bend the will of squirrels to her whim, had decided that she'd had just about enough of Lady Helene D'Orange's pet rooster waking the whole of their posh neighborhood before dawn. She had commanded these scores of beasts who lived in the trees of nearby Rhone Square to descend upon Lady Helen's yard.

"It was an unauthorized rooster. Urban zoning and all," the Prince was quick to point out. "And we'll have no fear of the Duchess repeating the same stunt again. I doubt any other neighbors would keep a rooster in the future. Lady Helene's hasn't been seen or heard from since."

I clenched my jaw shut against stronger reprimands, swallowing them along with my dignity. I was a grown man having an argument about enchanted squirrels.

"And still," I repeated. "Yours is an awful plan. Insisting that each squirrel she commands be officially registered and harnessed begs her to keep them as pets, which sounds to me like an engraved invitation to build a full militia."

The Prince kept his lips tight, but his eyes crinkled and sparkled in a way that let me know he had been having fun at my expense.

"Is this not a bureaucracy? And am I not the biggest and bureaucrattiest bureaucrat of them all?" He kept up the ruse. "She will stop this foolishness if we tie her with red tape."

"Yet you know that we must abide by the guidelines put

forth in the Ministry Rule of Law. It's all in Section Ten, Article Twelve, Letter F: *no animals may be harmed or confined in carrying out a disciplinary action.* Not to mention South Abarran law, which prohibits the ownership, sale, purchase, trafficking and domestication of rodents in the Sciuridae family.

He narrowed his eyes. "Seriously. How do you even know that?"

The truth was I didn't. But if he could be ridiculous, so could I. And the point wasn't *where* the rule was—it was that a similar rule existed and that the Prince really ought to be busy familiarizing himself with the Ministry's laws.

There were three ways to stop the ruling class from raining destruction with their powers. Prevention was presided over by the Ministry's regulatory arm. They took care of most of it—assessing, monitoring and explicitly dictating how supos were and weren't permitted to use their powers. Royals who had demonstrated problematic behavior were each assigned a case worker, mid-level employees who kept meticulous logs of abuses and speculated on worst-case scenarios should destruction be unleashed.

Scores of case workers clocked in every day, reporting to cubicles on the fourth-through-ninth floors. They were analysts and assessors of risk. But decisions about long-term sanctions needed sign-off by the minister. Handing out punishments to an entitled, elite class who resented the Ministry and would complain was touchy work.

"Something must be done about the Duchess." My voice was quieter this time. I abandoned procedure and hoped to appeal to him on the basis of common sense. "This is not an isolated incident and squirrel-related havoc can become quite severe."

The Prince nodded, relenting. I saw the moment when he put all joking aside. "What would Duke Oleander do?"

"Duke Oleander is not the minister."

"Yet, he has made decisions in my stead when I have been out of pocket. And he is more experienced."

Was he looking for me to agree? Or was this another trick to get me out? I doubted the vulnerability I saw in his eyes.

"He, too, had to learn," I pointed out. "I ask but that you try."

"He is suited to the position, is he not? A follower of rules in a way that I never will be," the Prince pressed.

I bit my tongue against what I knew. This was the part of the job that I hated—part of what made me angry all the time. The Prince's rebelliousness doubled my workload. And I resented him for being so sexy. But I liked the part of him that didn't drive me bonkers. And I didn't like lying to him.

"We all have a role to play."

"Easy to say for a man who was called to do exactly this." The Prince's voice went low. "Consider yourself lucky that you cannot fathom the call of a power such as we royals have. To be separated from such an instinct is a curse. It is visceral—the instinct to nurture one's power as a father nurtures his child."

"No." I lied through my teeth. "I cannot imagine that."

CHAPTER FIVE

Xabier Oleander Zabala, Duke of Shrubs, son of Ezkerro Zabala and second cousin to me was twenty-third in line to the throne. He lived a solid hour outside of South Dulibre and commuted to the Ministry each day from an estate with gardens befitting his name. The half-timbered, half-stone-built residence with its gently sloping roofs remained true to the style of the region. Though stately in size and upkeep, its lines were undramatic and—like Ollie's personality—the building was a bit bland.

The gardens were its saving grace—its pièce de résistance, the crown jewel of the property and Ollie's pride and joy. It was where he hosted guests on the rare spring occasion when he entertained. There were three, each with a different theme: one completely full of oleander, with its oranges and reds and whites and yellows and pinks; closest to the residence was the topiary garden, which featured only Alice in Wonderland-themed trimmings; at the far end of his property was the third garden—the maze.

"Delighted that you've come for a visit," Ollie remarked

jovially. "It's seldom that we have a chance to see one another outside of work."

"I'm afraid my social life is lacking these days," I admitted truthfully. "Plus, opposite shifts, and all. Do you still see Vitts?"

I asked after the closest cousin-friend we'd always had in common. He and Vittoria were first cousins, but she and I were closer in age.

"Not much, I'm afraid," Ollie admitted. "Second shift and all."

If there was anyone who I should have felt sorrier for than I felt for myself, it was Ollie. It was only for the lucky fact he actually enjoyed the job that I didn't. Even with the hours he worked, he performed with relish and did not complain.

"Plus," he continued. "She's none too diligent about keeping her little habit in check and she knows I'm by the book."

I couldn't help but to chuckle at that. Vittoria had the power of mimicry. She was like a walking sound effects machine. That, combined with a wicked sense of humor, made for great fun at parties and in crowds. She'd won me over at the tender age of ten, when she'd convinced our entire class that a boy who bullied me had an incurable case of flatulence. She'd even gotten our distant cousin, who could create spontaneous smells, in on the joke.

As an adult, she'd only somewhat settled down. In the company of those who knew of her power, she was still good for crickets during awkward silences and other such smartassery. Get her in a room full of strangers, and she really had her fun.

"I must admit," I began slowly, "that I quite envy your reputation as an enforcer. You do your post an honor inasmuch as you are known for being steadfast."

My cousin seemed distressed by my self-deprecation. "You are in a difficult position," he replied. "Few other than ourselves are burdened to know the stressors of the job. As the Minister, all actions done by people within the agency—good or bad—fall upon you."

"Duke Grimaud handled things far more gracefully, I'm afraid."

"Duke Grimaud had two-and-a-half decades on the job before he passed on," Ollie countered. "Even with that experience, he did not leave the Ministry in good regard."

"Yet you have been a constant force, behind the scenes, lending your wisdom and skill to the running of the Ministry, without receiving an ounce of credit. It is no secret that it is you who was expected to have been appointed to the post I was granted."

Duke Oleander's response was predictably neutral. "Men of duty can harbor no expectations."

"Come now, there must be more to it than that."

We were not so close that I expected him to speak freely without a bit of prodding. The Duke seemed to carefully weigh his words.

"Had Queen Maialen called upon me to fulfill this duty, I would have done so without hesitation."

"Is it not the truth that you are qualified to be a better Minister than I?"

Ollie stopped in his tracks and turned his gaze to me in panic, his features a mix of horror and shame.

"Cousin—" he stammered as his face reddened and he grasped for a reply. What remaining doubt I'd held about his aspirations were eradicated by the look on his face. "I've never meant to ... if I've ever indicated..." I waited patiently for him to calm.

"I apologize if I have said or done anything to give the impression that I have designs on your role as Minister," he said shakily as he finally straightened himself. "I am, as ever and always, your humble servant."

"And for that, I am grateful. It is because of your humility, and your sense of duty that you have earned my trust. Can I trust you now to hold my confidence on an important matter? It is one that involves the both of us."

Ollie blinked again. "Of course, cousin. I can only hope that it is nothing dire."

I clasped my hands behind my back and resumed walking.

"I don't see any shame in having ambitions. Passion is the hallmark of all great men. When we care about something deeply, we excel. Look around us." I motioned my hands to indicate his sculptures which, despite his unfortunate choice of subject, were quite exquisite. "Only a passionate man could have invested the time—the sheer patience and precision—to create this."

Ollie was, as ever, sincere. "It doesn't feel like work. When I'm trimming, everything just ... flows."

"I'm told that you have demonstrated similar talents at the Ministry."

"What has been said of my talents there?"

"Not merely that you are diligent and efficient—that you have a natural talent for the work that can't be explained."

He quieted as we continued our walk.

"I will admit—I have seen it as well. Perhaps have even been jealous of it. You possess a passion that I lack. And though you have done nothing to indicate that you are anything less than loyal to me and your position, I can't help but to think that you may be better suited to the Minister of Powers position."

"You flatter me," Ollie said simply in a dejected sort of way.

"Then why do you sound so glum?"

"Because talents and passion can be cruel when pitted against expectations. Our duty is what it is. Some of us are lucky enough to see our duties coincide with that which we love. But many of us—like you and I—simply aren't."

His words rang so true that they threatened to throw me down a pit of melancholy. But I had to remember my task.

"What if we stopped leaving it up to luck?" I challenged. "What if—together—we could persuade Queen Maialen that we were each called to do something different?"

"But the Ministry... Queen Maialen has entrusted you with national security. I can only imagine that she has done so because she trusts you immensely. Can such preferences truly be second-guessed?"

"I am beginning to fear that my role as beloved nephew to our queen is clouding her judgment. It pains me to say that she may have overestimated me."

Ollie gazed at me in earnest as he gave his response. "You do yourself a disservice to speak of your abilities in this way. You are five years my junior—and six years less tenured within the Ministry. Now is still the time for you to learn."

"No, cousin," I corrected gently. "I do the country a disservice by not admitting when I am out of my depth. If the Queen overestimates me, it is my duty to let her know."

"Have you felt this way for a long while?"

We were just coming upon a table that had been left for us to sit at. It was set with small plates—local delicacies—and wine.

"I have raised the issue with the Queen before," I admitted.

"And what was her response?"

Ollie motioned for me to sit first. The table was in the shade of an enormous tree that had been trimmed in such a way that its canopy was the perfect rendition of an umbrella.

"Similar to yours, I'm afraid. The Queen believes that it is merely a matter of learning and not a matter of skill. I'm almost certain my lack of experience will do us harm. Just last week, Chester the Molester struck again, on my watch."

Chester the Molester was the common name we used for Sir Arthur Pinto, Earl of Ferulia, a randy teenager with the power to disrobe anybody he meant to by command of his thoughts.

"Good gods," Ollie blurted with distaste. His hand halted for a moment in mid-air, holding the napkin that had been en route to his lap. Both of us were now seated at the table.

"Seems someone's hot for teacher," I murmured cheekily.

"What was his punishment this time?" Ollie wanted to know.

"That's just it—it still hasn't been decided. Half the time, when a disciplinary decision is in my care, I'm told that policy would prohibit me from exacting justice in the way that I would prefer."

At this, Ollie gave a smile. It prompted me to ask, "What?"

"Swearing Salvador," he said with continued amusement. "Word is, you had him followed 'round by a launderer under orders to wash his mouth out with soap every time he used salty language."

"It was a good punishment," I insisted before murmuring, "even though it only lasted for a week. How did you find out about it?"

"Zain Otxoa," Ollie reported with an easy smile before popping a bite of sausage in his mouth and chewing thoroughly. "Not that he blabbered. Actually, he was quite discreet."

Famished after my long ride, I'd had it in mind to take my own bite, but something inside me went cold at his words. Which part unnerved me more? That my adversary had been loath to spread the details of our tense exchange or that my cousin knew him casually? I decided, in a second, that it was both.

"And what did he tell you?" Unlike Mr. Otxoa, I was not discreet.

"That you were still learning and that once he informed you of allowable punishments per the procedural manuals, that you were able to choose a more appropriate penalty."

I did take a bite of sausage then, mostly to stall myself from talking. For as much trouble as I gave him, I was certain that

Zain Otxoa would curse me to high heaven, with a vitriol that rivaled the skills of Salvador himself. I had never heard explicitly that he badmouthed me, but even if I had, I would not have reprimanded him for it. Anything he said about me was likely to be true, and well-deserved.

"I hear this is a vintage you enjoy?"

Without me having to say a word, Ollie picked up the wine which my people had insinuated to his people that I would very much like to see on the table. For men in my position, the indulgence of one's particularities was commonplace.

"Yes..." I watched him pour the Ichor, enjoying the process of seeing the liquid fall into the glass. Its color was the perfect mix of amethyst and ruby. Even without tasting it, I could smell it faintly and I enjoyed the way it awakened my senses with just one whiff.

"Have you tried the Ichor before?" I baited.

Ollie gaped in disbelief. "Have I?" he repeated, more comfortable now. "You won't believe what I had to do to snap up the ten cases I got. It's magic in a bottle."

We toasted silently and I drank first, as was the custom. I watched him as he readied himself to take his sip. I took immense enjoyment from the expression on his face as he tasted.

"You do know that I have more than a sporting interest when it comes to wine," I baited again.

"Duke of Brix and all," he came back easily.

I took a slow sip and put my glass down. It gave me pause to know that he would be the first who I told. Even the workers in Fesik's vineyards did not suspect the true reasons for my presence on his estate.

"What would you do if I told you that it was I who made this wine? That I've made wine all along? And that all of it has been against the orders of Queen Maialen?"

Ollie put down his glass and raised an eyebrow.

"That I sincerely hope that you do not get caught. Partially for your own sake in avoiding her wrath, and also for the sake of our country. It would be a tragedy, to lose wine like this."

"I cannot think of any greater evidence of my true calling," I said in earnest. "And I truly believe the Ministry is yours. And I believe that we could each find our way to doing what we were meant to, with some convincing."

"What do you propose?" He asked with more caution than conspiracy.

"Talk badly about me," I said simply. "Tell anyone who has the ear of Queen Maialen that I am unsuited to my job. On my end, I will sing your praises and speak bluntly to the Queen about my doubts. She will be left to conclude that you are the only choice as Minister. I will be released to my true calling—crafting wine."

PART II
THE QUEEN

CHAPTER SIX

Zain

"You're late," Sylvain informed me with the sort of wicked glee that always seemed etched on his face and bled into his not-deep voice. It was too low to be considered high, but only just. "I've gotten your uniform out of the bag," he continued, plucking a hanger displaying the offending garment off of the top edge of the locker room door. "Though I'd say this one is more of a costume. What little there is of it, eh?"

I took the proffered hanger and turned it slightly, holding it far away from my body so as not to be poked in the eye by an angel wing. "Not a lot to it" was an understatement. The white booty shorts were the only garment that would offer even a shred of discretion. Tonight's event was a charity fashion show dinner with a *Paradise Lost* theme.

"For a person who doesn't need to keep my server job, I'm right on time," I came back with lightness. Arriving here was the best thing that had happened to me all day.

"Tell that to the party manager. She's a bit high-strung. And she's been down here looking for you twice. Something about needing to have you dressed twenty minutes ago so she can hustle you on to glitter."

I threw him a look that told him that even I had limits. "I will not allow myself to be glittered."

"Ah-ah..." he tutted. "Rule number one of being an intervenor is to blend in. Being glittered is part of the job."

I scowled at Sylvain's black suit. Whereas my part to play tonight was that of a waiter, his was as a security guard. Sylvain was brawnier than me. And with his skill—encyclopedic recollection of all living royals with registered powers— he was well-suited to being first to see who walked in.

Most Saturday nights, he and I were paired together. Dealing with rogue supos—or even those who might become so—was no solitary endeavor. Intervenors were a necessary precaution against an indelible fact: sometimes prevention failed. We were boots on the ground, inserting ourselves into the action. It was part anticipation, part de-escalation. It was what I was born to do.

"Rule number one of intervening is to be present at the right moment with precisely the correct skill," I came back.

Not to be confused with royal powers, "skills" were what we called the abilities possessed by people like Sylvain and me. Our powers were not registered and our royal lineage was muddy and obscured. We roamed the world as commoners and concealed our skills for various reasons. Some of us—like me—wound up working for the Ministry's covert arm.

Masquerading as a waiter was the best way for me to use my skill. It gave me unfettered access to most people in the room. Everybody needed to be offered something, or served something, or to have a plate or glass removed discreetly. Most of all, it was easy to escape scrutiny. Nobody looked at you when you were the help.

Ten minutes later, I had donned my get-up, persuaded the party manager that I had plenty of natural sparkle, and begun serving drinks for an uneventful first hour. The Ministry rated the gatherings it believed to be the highest risk. Friday and Saturday nights were when people got wild.

"Mocktails for the Marquess of Marlo. She's got that look in her eye," I announced as I sidled up to the bar. It wasn't as easy as it looked considering my wings. The Marquess enjoyed preventing people from lying a bit too much. It sent liars tripping over their tongues and blurting out nonsense that made for comic relief. It wasn't the same as being able to force people to tell the truth. That one had been wielded by the late and much-missed Duchess of Ravenna, whose timing had been nothing short of masterful. I liked that about this job. It was more entertaining than Broadway theater. And I couldn't *not* do it. I loved the rush.

"What was she having?" the bartender, Traci, asked, stifling a yawn. Not much was happening yet.

"Gin and tonic." I watched as she poured the drink. First, the liquor and mixer—all of it full strength—then squeezed in her magic in tandem with squeezing in the lime. Traci had the ability to cleanse any substance of alcohol, all while making sure it tasted exactly the same. Her skill to not let royals get quite so drunk had averted much trouble at many such events.

I thought briefly to remark that the night was turning out to be a bore, then reconsidered. Nothing invited a good jinx better than daring the universe to prove you wrong.

"Trouble at five o'clock."

I was discreet enough not to turn too quickly. When I did, I saw the smug mug of Arlo Gris, Marquis of La Paix, just inside the entryway to the hall. Greeting his way into the room, he was all smiles, nods and winks. Arlo had an appeal that I had never understood. His power—charm—had always felt quite plastic to me. But he was like catnip to women.

At this very moment, he had a woman on his arm—predictably young and naïve to what was about to occur.

"Maite's gotten wind of him." Traci's voice broke into my consciousness at the exact moment that my eyes slid to Arlo's first ex-wife.

My eyes darted next to Koralina Bey, born a commoner, now the Duchess of Sechy—also, Arlo's ex-wife number two. Her second husband, the Duke of Sechy, was a more suitable choice for a husband, and made up in character what he lacked in looks.

"Kora's seen him, too," I reported back to Traci for good measure. The way Kora still looked at Arlo made me feel sorry for the guy.

"She's not the one you ought to be worried about."

Diana Rute was ex-wife number three and she stood across the room, clearly incensed.

Hell hath no fury, indeed, I mused, shifting my attention to Sylvain, who had abandoned his post at the door and was already cutting his way through the crowd.

"Who is she?" I asked when he reached me, inclining my head to the girl on Arlo's arm.

"Not in our files." He continued to scan the room. "If she's a supo or a half-blood, she's not registered."

"She's barely legal," Traci murmured with a bit of disgust.

"Maite won't like that." I turned back toward the bar to make it less obvious that we were plotting. "Last time I saw them together, Arlo told her she was looking a little long in the tooth."

"Why? 'Cause she's over twenty-five?" Traci still sounded disgusted. She herself looked to be about that age.

"What's his third wife's power?" I turned slightly to Sylvain. "All I remember is that Maite can make things bigger."

Sylvain suddenly looked haunted. "That's one I've worked hard to forget. The things I saw in the emergency room that night cannot be unseen."

Even I had to shudder at the recollection. When Arlo had

pulled the same stunt before, parading Kora around at an affair attended by Maite, she'd used her power to make his phallus uncomfortably large. The doctors said it was the worst case they had ever seen. When questioned about her motives, all Maite had said was that if Arlo had such a big boner for younger women, that getting him off would be her wedding gift to he and his latest wife.

"Is she still under review for that offense?" I wanted to know. "Under review" was a nicer term we used with royals instead of saying they were on parole.

Sylvain nodded as he looked back out at the crowd. "For another year, but a reminder couldn't hurt. The Duke of Sechy looks a bit pissed too. But neither of them is our biggest risk."

"Diana," I concluded. She was the one who he had left only recently—the one for whom the abandonment would be fresh.

"She can cause any object that's not nailed down to a surface to fall," Sylvain chimed back in. "A parlor trick on a good day. Only, today isn't very good."

Property damage was a common consequence of abused powers gone wrong. But bodily harm seemed a possibility. Most situations gone sideways involved powers used to lash out in fits of passion. Diana could make obstacles fall in front of them to trip them where they walked.

"I'll take Kora first."

I picked up my tray, set to deliver my long-ready set of drinks. A swell of excitement rose in my chest. There was a delicious adrenaline to all of this. Moments like this made it worth it—moments that made me feel free and alive and that let me be who I truly was. After all of the pretending I did, day-to-day, in a mundane world that didn't know the truth about me, I had this.

Bypassing the table that had ordered the drinks on my tray, I made a beeline for the Duke and Duchess of Sechy, whose table was closest to the bar. If I got just a bit too close and set the drinks down in just the right place, the person whose space I had invaded would look.

"Thinking about starting a scuffle with the Marquis?" I questioned the Duke of Sechy.

My questions were always this abrupt. In order for my skill to work, a seed had to be planted.

"What did you say?" the Duke demanded.

"Do yourself a favor," I instructed in a stern voice. "Don't."

The Duchess had been too transfixed by her ex to notice our brief exchange. Though she possessed no extraordinary powers, she was still capable of havoc.

"You seem quite taken by the Marquis of Le Paix, Your Grace," I remarked, plunking down a flute of somebody else's champagne. I waited for eye contact and knew I would get it after setting the glass down too hard. Then, I spoke my command: "Sit placidly as you continue to succumb to his charm."

With that done, I stalked off, beating a path across the room to Diana's location. She studied the meandering couple with ire. It wasn't clear whether she had something planned for Arlo or something planned for the girl. She looked angry enough that she might have had plans for both.

Upon reaching where she sat alone, I placed my body in front of hers. Breaking her gaze might break her concentration. Placing the second to last of my drinks in front of her on the table, I was in such a hurry that it sloshed. I squatted down until I was looking her directly in the eye.

"You want to hurt both of them, don't you?"

She blinked in surprise at my voice. She hadn't even seen me.

"Don't bother. He's not worth the consequences, and you ought to have compassion for the girl. One day, she'll be like you."

With that, I made a split for the final table—the one with

Arlo's first wife, Maite, who seemed closer to bad decisions than she had been a moment before.

"Thinking of violating your review period?" I asked, weaving a bit in front of her until she looked me in the eye. When she did, I issued my final declaration. "No using your powers tonight. Not on him."

As I spoke to Maite, recognition dawned. She knew what I was doing because I had done it to her before. Only, she could just recall it for a split second and wouldn't remember any of this the next day.

By the time I reached Arlo himself, I had no more drinks on my tray and nothing to offer but words.

"Do not attempt to charm me," I started right in.

He blinked. The woman looked at him.

"Thought you would have a little fun with your ex-wives, did you? Party's over. It's time to go home."

"You can't kick us out of here," the woman said to me, and then, to him, "What does he mean, ex-*wives*?"

But I didn't need to stick around for the explanation. I also didn't need to watch him leave to know that he would. I had done my magic—crisis averted. All was safe and well. I let down my tray and returned to my duties at the bar. The high that came in the wake of unleashing my skills thrummed through my body with vigor. It would buoy me for days.

CHAPTER SEVEN

Xabier
Queen Maialen was the grandest of dames, all elegance and regality and a tough old cookie to boot. She was the elder sister of my father, who was next in line to the throne after the Queen's own son. Barely in danger of inheriting the throne given the position of my cousin, Prince Zorian, my father spent most of his time doing as he pleased and gallivanting abroad.

I had always been fond of my Aunt Maialen and she quite fond of me. She had sent me into fits of laughter during our play when I was a child. Her power—to spawn fully functional ancillary copies of herself, a feat she could achieve as long as her clones were in her sight line—had given games like hide and seek and Marco Polo a smashing sense of fun.

"Your Majesty," I announced myself from thirty paces, not wanting to scare the old girl. I had caught her in the vineyards quite on purpose. My aunt was not the sort of queen to rule strictly from behind her desk, or seated atop her throne. She preferred to know the outside world—and, when not strictly doing that, to at least be outdoors.

"Out for your morning walk, I see," I remarked. It was early hours indeed. I had awakened before the sun to make my way to her palace. I prided myself on being one of very few individuals who could arrive for a visit to the Queen unannounced.

She stretched out her hand and I bowed, kissing her heavy ring, its jewel the color of a ripe pinot grape. I smirked when I stood upright and took in her lips, which were stained purple inside of her pucker. The Queen had been drinking wine.

"And you've had your morning nip," I murmured a bit cheekily. Such were things between us. In public, I followed the proper protocols of deference, honoring her station with my respect. In private, we were playful and there was much love.

"You know what I say about a cup of wine."

She reached into some hidden pocket of the cape she wore for warmth and produced a silver vessel, which she held out to me in offer. It wasn't the first time the Queen had shared her morning cup. The bejeweled flask was four times as heavy as any wine it might contain. I smiled less in thanks than anticipation. The quality of her morning libation would be the best of the best. After all, she was the queen.

I took a slow, shallow sip, all the better to savor its artistry. It was a celebration of sweetness and tannins in my mouth. It was honey and skins and the clay of the soil and alluvial flavors from rivers that flowed strong and constant centuries before I was born.

"Give me wine to wash me clean of the weather-stains of cares." I recited the Emerson quote. I'd heard her speak the words on more occasions than I could count. Her morning drink did seem to rejuvenate her somehow. She was sharp and clear-minded even after a good, deep cup.

"And what of your cares, my child? Oughtn't you be at the Ministry?"

I passed back her wine. She took a long sip before replacing the lid and hiding the flask in some pocket or hidden compartment within her cloak.

"Actually, I'm quite confident being away. The Duke of Shrubs has proven himself to be quite capable. He's been trustworthy to a fault and well-suited to the work."

"The Duke of Shrubs..." the Queen repeated, as if trying to recall the name.

"Oleander Zabala, son of Ezkerro Zabala. He's my second in command. Four years my senior, though he's worked at the Ministry for five years longer than I."

"Ezkerro Zabala's son..." A sour note came into the Queen's voice as she spoke of the Duke of Dariouche, known impolitely as the Prince of Thieves. The man lacked scruples, to be sure.

"I hope that his moral compass is better-oriented than his father's." The Queen rarely spoke ill so openly.

My voice softened and I paused my walk long enough to quote Emerson once again. "Cannot we let children be themselves, and enjoy life in their own way?"

Aunt Maialen paused as well and gazed up at me with a pensive look. Her lips turned up in a small, sad smile.

"Quite right," she conceded, reaching out her hand to place it on my arm. "The Duke has become for you a great lieutenant. For that, I am glad."

We resumed our walk, turning a corner after having reached the end of a row. The path would take us west, through more rows until we reached a blooming garden.

"He has been more than my lieutenant."

Now it was the Queen's turn to stop.

"Oh?" she asked with interest.

I nearly balked at the implication. The Duke of Shrubs neither shared my proclivities nor was he my type. I was quick to protest the notion, though I made the correction as gently as one must do, even with the most familiar of monarchs.

"Professionally, my queen. He has been invaluable to me. I fear that he is underutilized."

"Is there not some higher post you are able to give him? Even if only in name?"

"There is one position that would work quite well."

"And?" The Queen seemed to sense some complexity.

"The ideal position for the Duke would be mine."

The Queen did not stop walking this time—only kept on with her slow stroll. I kept quiet, knowing better than to push. It seemed a simple enough matter, but her response took longer than I anticipated. Her answer required no mention of anything I had rehearsed.

"I cannot allow you to vacate your post."

The quietude of her words did nothing to lessen their sting. My mind and heart erupted with the one question that even a beloved nephew could not ask of his queen. She insisted that I stay. But why?

In the sanctuary of my private consciousness, I had long-since accepted the stark truth: I was educated, yes, and competent in some general, unimpressive way. But people were good at things they loved. Which explained why I was so bad at signing off on things and reading lengthy reports.

"I cannot help but to think that there are other ways for me to be of service. If not a complete abandonment of my post, perhaps a scaling-back? Certainly, Majesty, it is my intention to do my duty. But I have wondered how well the vineyards might do were they to receive my help."

I stopped again, stepped closer to a vine, and placed my hand beneath a cluster, holding my breath for a beat before I allowed the energy to flow. Even for a small display such as this, allowing the energy to release felt divine. And that was just the intoxication of the outflow—also spectacular was the result: a single cluster, ripened to perfection by my touch.

Exhilaration still welled in my chest as I plucked off one

exemplary grape. We stood now in a field of Rousanne. It was bruised and beautiful and something within me didn't want to let it go. Yet, I passed it to the Queen with expectation, and with a boldness no other would have dared to attempt. Remnants of my power still coursed through my body, making me high.

The Queen took the proffered grape, but kept her attention on to me, scrutinizing me somehow.

"It's come of age," she murmured, yet she didn't touch the grape. "Your power," she further explained.

Only, the Queen knew that I had been using my power since I was a child.

"It's gotten stronger, Majesty, if that's what you mean." I thought of Fesik's words. "Though, I do sometimes wish that it could be put to better use. More frequently, it seems insistent that I let it out."

"Your power is of tremendous import, Xabier."

It was rare for her to use my given name. She looked at me so intensely that I stuttered out my answer. "Y-yes, your Majesty. I believe it is as well. I want to honor your country. Won't you allow me to make wine?"

I nodded to the fruit that still sat between her fingers, holding it out in encouragement for her to have a taste. Breathlessly, I awaited her reaction.

"Is it not perfect, Majesty?" I could not help but ask. Yet, her face gave it all away. She closed her eyes and ignored me, her lips upturned in a wide smile as she chewed. The small act transformed her and—for just a few seconds—she looked like a little girl tasting chocolate for the very first.

I waited with satisfied patience, vindicated somehow but troubled all the same.

"Indeed, it is," she began to say before she even opened her eyes. "And indeed, you are." She fixed her gaze on me kindly. "And I wish I could spare you now. But things are afoot at the

Ministry—things that need strong leadership and capable hands."

I thought of the rumors that Duke Oleander had assured me that he had started—not even rumors, merely unvarnished truths. I had upheld my end of the bargain by singing the Duke's praises to all who would listen. The Queen had many eyes and many lieutenants. It was unlikely that she would not have heard our titterings. The longer she remained steadfast, the more I wondered at what hidden factors drove her position.

"Is there something wrong with The Duke of Shrubs? Something unsavory or untoward?" Despite her earlier questioning, I was certain she knew who he was.

"Not at all," she assured. "There is something right with you."

But what of my wine?

I thought to ask it, then thought again given my doubt that I could spit out the question without a pout and a whiny protest. Because Queen Maialen was a far more astute leader than me, she answered the question I hadn't asked.

"If you insist upon making wine, use the process only to push the boundaries of your skill."

It was an odd comment, but one that I would not reject. It answered nothing but gave permission. It kept me from what I wanted, and added to the list of things that I did not understand.

CHAPTER EIGHT

Zain

Sunday nights were early nights that came off of sluggish days. I's were best-dotted and T's best-crossed when details were fresh. A good soak in the tub and a nice bottle of wine as my reward each Sunday night gave way to perfect rest and languorous Mondays that found me sleeping well into afternoon.

Wake up.

Some unwelcome instinct broke into my thoughts and tried to coax me from blissful sleep. A far more sensible instinct told that instinct to shut up. Asleep or awake, lounging in my own bed was delicious. Technically, I had a few of my own beds in the pied-à-terres that I kept across South Abarra as I worked my various jobs. But this was my very best bed in my favorite house.

And wouldn't it be nice to share it?

This one was a different voice—the one that came to me every Monday morning once I was half-awake, lounging exactly like this. Dreams that I sincerely wished that I could remember gave way to imaginings that were difficult not to ignore when I had no place to be on time and appendages that were needy and stiff.

It should have bothered me that in my one place of refuge —so far away from the city and from the responsibilities that stole my time—he reached me still. That notions of sharing a bed and relieving my ache led to fantasies of sapphire eyes. I would do now as I had done every Monday—indulge it with relish and remind myself that I, too, deserved joyous moments. I would wait until I had at least one cup of coffee before judging myself for my infatuation with the Prince.

Wake up.

When that voice spoke again, a full return to sleep seemed unlikely. Still groggy, I rolled to the left, pulling the covers tighter over myself with my top hand as I set to crack open my eyes. Off of the left side of the bed were double doors that opened to the sea in the distance and the vineyards below. It was my favorite view in the house; one I liked so much, I made sure to enjoy it each time I was in my home. Readying myself to enjoy what I was set to do with my lower hand, I breathed in a soft gasp as I touched what drove my urgency. I opened my eyes to see where I had put my lube.

"Queen Maialen!"

Before I shouted the words in alarm, I made a loud, desperate noise—one I was fairly sure sounded like a locked-trunk magician coming up from the water and gasping for air. The next thing I knew, I was sitting up in my bed. When I realized that doing so exposed my naked form—my front was covered with blankets pooled around me but the air on my back and the tops of my buttocks were cool from the morning breeze—I lay back down. I vainly wished that whatever stiffness had been present just moments before would turn limp at a greater pace.

"I apologize, Your Majesty."

When my eyes had first fallen upon her, her back had

been too me, her hair blowing lightly in the briny morning breeze. I supposed, through my reaction, I had only myself to blame for the sort of attention I was receiving now. Though she didn't seem to mind. In truth, she looked amused by my predicament. Maialen was that kind of queen.

"Whatever for? It is I who projected a copy of myself into your bedroom."

It partially answered a question I would have needed to find a delicate way to ask.

"I'm waiting downstairs in my car. I came up simply to coax you awake and ask to be let in."

"My apologies, Majesty. I didn't hear the bell."

It felt beyond odd to be speaking to the Queen as I lay on my back with my covers up to my neck.

She gave a knowing smile before disappearing. "I believe you were in the midst of a very deep sleep, and a very good dream."

∽

"His time is near," Queen Maialen proclaimed after a single sip of tea, taken in my sitting room downstairs—not shabby by any stretch, but not quite fit for a queen. The doors leading outside were open to a lower deck of dark, lacquered wood that also overlooked the vineyard hills.

"I received a visit from the Prince early this morning," she continued. "He was frenetic about using his powers. He would like me to excuse him from his post so that he can make wine. It was all through his own interpretation, but I am certain. He is beginning to feel the change."

The Queen and I had had several such conversations about several royals in similar positions—charges who were similar to the Prince in theory but who hardly seemed similar at all.

Usually, it was I who came to the Queen with news of readiness and she who voiced her reservations.

"I defer to you, Majesty," I began, as I was in no position to do the latter. "But I do feel obliged to tell you that I have yet to witness such a change. Your Highness knows what would happen if we were to proceed without supreme confidence that the Prince was ready."

The weight of her answering sigh was proof that she wasn't sure.

"If he feels a change within himself, I am inclined to trust it, even if it is a change that we cannot see. I fear equally for what will come of us if we proceed as we have been."

"You are correct, Majesty." I said it as agreeably as possible.

"Yet you harbor lingering doubt."

I cringed as I confessed. "I do, Your Majesty. Before we proceed, I would like to see it myself."

"What do you propose, Mr. Otxoa?"

I thought of other occasions when I had been unsure.

"Perhaps I could arrange a test."

∽

"Could you please notify His Majesty that I am waiting on the rear car park, ready for our ride-along?"

Eusebio said nothing for a long moment before voicing the tart, "Hold, please," that he liked to default to any time he was consulting the Prince. He returned in half a minute. "The Prince does not recall discussing any such appointment. A ride-along with who, exactly?"

"A ride-along with me," I said as innocently as possible. "I mentioned it to the Prince when we last met. Article 5, Section 3a of the handbook specifically mentions that all high officials are intended to attend ride-alongs at least quarterly to keep their knowledge of current events fresh."

I held my breath in the silence, waiting to see whether Eusebio would take the story at face value. Unlike the Prince, he actually read the manuals. The more I thought about my fake policy, the better an idea it sounded. Ridealongs weren't glamorous, but they were a good way to learn.

Just as I was beginning to think that Eusebio had left me on hold for too long and that maybe I'd better ride up to the executive suite, the passenger door opened abruptly and the Prince climbed in. He held an air of compliance. He and I both knew that if I had announced the plan earlier, he would have found a way out. Perhaps the Queen was correct that the Prince was slowly opening himself to this work—slowly and unwittingly inching toward his rightful place.

"Good afternoon, Your Grace. Ready to experience a typical day in the life of a beat officer, I see..."

"Yes, well..." He looked out the window as I began to drive. "Now seems as good a time as any to apply myself. Guarding the security of the realm is, after all, my life's calling."

I had no inkling of what had been discussed between the Prince and the Queen. His tone proved that it had not gone well. His latest scheme, as I had surmised, was to install Duke Oleander. I felt for him then. It hadn't been a bad plan and under less dire circumstances, it would have worked. Had I been in his shoes, I might have tried the same maneuver myself.

"We all lead many lives," I responded quietly, not quite knowing what boldness compelled me to do so. "It has been my experience that contentment can be found, even in lives we do not choose."

I expected the Prince to say nothing in return—expected our entire trip to be silent, save from the instruction I would have to give to keep up the ruse.

My hidden plan was simple: to take the Prince on the most straightforward of calls, for which a resolution would be abundantly clear—calls involving minor predicaments that could be fixed without powers. Minor events that would begin teasing his instincts were the perfect place to start.

"Yet it is obvious that you were born to do this—to lead the Ministry as you do. Its halls are a place that you never leave. You are the embodiment of the job, right down to arriving first in the morning and leaving last, and tucking that pencil you like behind your ear."

I said nothing at first, bewildered. The Prince had given me thought? He had looked into my comings and goings? Never once had I expected that he would look beyond what I demanded of him. I'd chalked up the times he'd seemed to notice me to wishful thinking.

"I'm not at the Ministry now, am I?"

"No..." The Prince began slowly. "But we are on Ministry business. You are thorough and circumspect when it comes to your job. You take it seriously. There is something in your way of approaching your work that is rarely seen. It is a sort of caring."

I could have said nothing, or nodded, or even thanked him for his comment, but I did not. "It is how I know that you will be a splendid Minister one day, my lord," I remarked after a short minute. "Contrary to what you might like others to believe, I can see that you care as well."

Before the softness in the silence that stretched between us could tempt me to utter another word, the radio crackled with news that we had a call. I had spoken to dispatch, who were given very specific instructions to only route through certain kinds of incidents.

"Dispatch to unit 4-1-5, we have a juvenile male at Diallo Elementary who's disturbed the peace at band practice. The original motive seems to have been a prank. He's spun up a polka situation in which the impacted victims are powerless to stop themselves from playing folk tunes. Are you able to answer the call? Over."

I plucked up the radio as I drove and pressed a button on the repeater.

"4-1-5 to dispatch. We are en route and able to answer the call. Over."

"Thank you for confirmation, 4-1-5. We have you down to respond to the job. Call in for backup at any time if needed. Over and out."

By the time I replaced the repeater where it had been, the Prince looked over at me, a bit agog. "How do you handle a situation like that?"

"A badge and a uniform does the trick with adults," I answered honestly. "Intimidation factor and all. But children aren't always in control of their power. You can usually tell the ones making mischief from the ones who are truly in trouble. You never lost control of your power when you were a kid?"

The Prince looked thoughtful as he shook his head. "Not that I remember."

"How old were you? The first time?"

These were the kinds of things that weren't in the Prince's file. His memories. The mysteries behind his bright eyes.

His features softened and all of the resignation he'd carried when he'd climbed into the car faded. He smiled. "I don't know. Maybe three or four."

"That's younger than usual," I murmured.

"It was in my family vineyards..." His voice was softer and lower at the same time. "Trailing after our winemaker. He always let me come with him into the fields. I wasn't really helping—just tagging along. I liked to touch the clusters and duck in and out around the vines.

"That first time, the grapes on the vine looked ripe. I wanted to have some, for a snack. I was used to picking what I wanted from any of the trees and bushes on our land."

"What happened?"

I knew he would go on, but I was impatient to hear what came next. I thought of what he might have looked like as a little boy.

He smiled wistfully. "The grapes I tasted were bitter. But I was hungry. I wanted them to be sweet enough to eat."

"So you made them sweet enough to eat..." I concluded. "But how did you know you did? Or did you not understand it until later?"

"No..." he mused. "I think I did understand it then. But I didn't think it was a big deal. When you're a kid, everything feels more magical."

"How did it feel to use it?" I asked, hoping to learn more about how his power worked, or at least coax him into connecting with its essence. Maybe going back to the beginning could help him invoke it now.

"It didn't feel like anything. It felt like I wanted the grapes to be sweeter, and then they were."

It spoke to a specific style. Unlike my power—which was driven by will—his was driven by instinct. It could prove difficult to draw his extended abilities out of him.

"Only, it didn't happen spontaneously..." I baited. "It was in line with your intention. You wanted something and the universe provided. Why did you want sweetened grapes so badly?"

He looked over at me and gave an impish smile. "Because they're delicious and eating them makes me happy."

Fifteen minutes later, we walked through the doors of Diallo Elementary and followed our ears to the sound, the beating of up-tempo drums and the blare of brass instruments leading our way. I watched the Prince carefully. I was always watching the Prince, but I scanned for signs of a visceral reaction.

The din became terrible as we approached the music room.

The style of music didn't suit me and was made only worse by the undeveloped skills of the young children who played.

"Grating, is it not?" I baited.

"Indeed," the Prince agreed with a wince. "I hope you're right about our badges. Somebody ought to make it stop."

Even as we walked closer, I listened carefully. Even if the Prince remained oblivious to his own power, there was a chance that, subconsciously, he would turn it down. But the volume of the awful music stayed the same.

"Why are they playing so loud?" the Prince asked a moment later. He didn't go so far as to plug his ears with his fingers, but looked rather like he wanted to.

"Unclear," I hollered truthfully.

As we stormed into the music room, I scanned for the offending child. Chairs were arranged around a conductor's platform in rainbow formation. The boy who seemed to be behind it all sat in the brass section three seats in from the end of a row, tears streaming down his cheeks and saxophone in hand. A teacher who had sandwiched his way into the row looked put-out and reproachful but nonetheless attempted to comfort the child as he began to cry.

As for the other children, they continued to play, clearly outside of their own volition, their hands moving strangely over buttons, drumsticks, and keys and finger holes. Two looked angry. One looked a bit distressed but the others laughed uproariously. Abarran children were resilient and acculturated to such interruptions as those with powers came of age. Anything that achieved distraction from the humdrum of school was generally thought of as a perk.

"How shall we help him?" I quizzed the Prince, giving him one more try. I would have to put a stop to this, though I would be very careful to ensure that he didn't see.

"He seems panicked," the Prince observed. For the moment,

we were still at a distance. "Perhaps if we can just calm him down, he can make himself stop."

The Prince's approach was viable, and I couldn't help but wonder whether this played at some true instinct or whether he had begun to read the manual after all.

Xabier forged forward, seeking no further consult from me and throwing a dashing smile and a small wave to the crowd. Children had begun to notice him. Even with their instruments in hand, those who seemed to recognize him humbled themselves with shallow bows.

I watched as he greeted the offending child, and then the child's teacher. He told them who we were and that we were there to help. Even over the din, Xabier spoke to the child in soothing tones. Something in the way he did it validated every bet the Queen had made on him. He could be good at this.

I watched, transfixed, as he lifted the child onto his lap and swung his legs to the side, instructing the boy to conjure in his mind a picture of the music stopping. Xabier sat calmly and told him to imagine peace and quiet. He even told the boy to imagine himself safe at home tucked into his own bed. He was so convincing that I half-expected it to work. I began to see that it wouldn't.

I knew what I needed to do. I approached the child and, for appearance's sake, chose words that gave the sense that I was only echoing the Prince—as if two of us on the job would be better than one. To avoid suspicion, I made sure that my first few phrases did nothing. When I thought it was safe enough, I spoke the words that would put all of it to an end.

"It's okay," I said aloud. "You can stop this. We're going to get you through."

∾

The free ice cream debacle—our second call that day—didn't go much better. Midweek, midday shenanigans were usually caused by kids. Little Lord Gilbert had the power to make any spigot keep flowing once it had been turned on. Every few months, the lordling hatched an elaborate attack on the village creamery with his friends. It usually involved deception to trick his governess, a clandestine escape from his family estate, and a meet-up with said friends at said creamery at a designated hour. The store workers never realized what was happening until it was too late, with soft serve flowing out of control.

"This is brilliant," the Prince remarked with excitement as we pulled up to the curb in front of the store, which spilled over with eager hordes of children at and around the door. The less fortunate of freeloaders ate from the smallish cones and paper cups supplied by the establishment. The more opportunistic children—likely the ones who were in on it or had caught word early on—ate from enormous mixing bowls brought in from home.

"The property damage will be enormous," I baited, curious to see what threats would sway the Prince. In order for his powers to emerge, he had to want to remedy what he saw as wrong.

"I'm thinking, by now, the damage is probably done," he observed.

Xabier inclined his chin toward two uniformed workers, one who sat with his back to the store, weeping helpless tears, the other with her arm around him, looking over her shoulder to watch the unfolding mischief.

"This sort of thing doesn't reflect well upon the Ministry," I dug in, hoping he cared at least a little about that.

"How old did you say the young lord was?" The Prince's gaze stayed out the window and he seemed to be scanning the crowd.

"Nine, if I recall correctly. He could be ten now."

Xabier turned back toward me with a conspiratorial smile. "Can't blame a ten-year-old kid for wanting a bit of fun."

Without another word, the Prince exited the car, breaking our seal of relative silence. Pandemonium awaited us outside—a cacophony of excited screams, accusations of budging in line and delighted praise for the young lord. I extricated myself from the car quickly and trotted after him. A swell of hope rose in my chest as the children parted to let him into the store. Was it some extension of his powers emerging or was it simple charisma? The din of excitement quieted as he walked in, causing me to wonder the same.

"Which one of you is Lord Gilbert?"

The crowd parted again, to reveal a pair of tweens sharing a banana split out of the hull of a model Viking ship that looked antique and that had certainly been stolen from some display. Across from the young Lord, to whom I threw a look of reproach out of sheer habit, sat a young girl who looked a bit too old and a bit too pretty for him.

"Prince Xabier," the boy murmured, beginning to stand. Xabier raised his hand in a manner meant to instruct the boy to stay seated.

"On a date, I see," the Prince remarked next, regarding the girl.

"Your Grace." The girl bowed her head and blushed, regarding him admiringly from beneath thick lashes.

"Created a bit of havoc, have we?" The Prince motioned his hand around the store. He didn't wait for an answer. "I think you'd better offer your apologies and see to it that all of this gets cleaned up."

The constant humming of the soft serve machines dispensing ice cream could be heard as they continued to pour.

"Yes, my lord," the child said, still half-frozen with fear. It was an unexpected response—one quite different from earlier responses we'd seen from the young lord from lesser civil servants. The test itself was going differently than I expected, by virtue of Xabier being such a high prince.

"I expect this to be sorted out by sunset—not just you, but your henchmen," the Prince commanded, motioning to several boys around his age behind the counter, who had been busy serving it up. The Prince leaned closer, in a way that seemed like it was meant to be menacing. "Sundown," he repeated before leaning back. "For now, can carry on."

An hour later, I was scowling as we pulled away from the curb of the store. The Prince licked happily at soft serve chocolate out of a waffle cone. After delivering the softest justice I had ever witnessed, the Prince had rolled up his sleeves, gone behind the counter and actually helped to serve the ice cream. The assembly line formed by the children behind the counter —clearly accomplices of the lordling—was mediocre at best. The floor had begun to run with melted ice cream. It had only taken the Prince a minute to direct and organize them on how to optimize their operation to deliver their stolen goods with the highest possible efficiency and the least possible mess.

And it wasn't just in serving ice cream that he had excelled. He had fielded questions elegantly—some children asked whether he was a real prince—and he indulged their every request, from excesses of caramel sauce to mixing flavors to walking away with not one ice cream, but two. He spoke to the forlorn employees of the store, informing them of the clean-up by sundown plan, giving them his card should they have any trouble, and emptying his billfold into the glass jar by the abandoned register—an astonishing sum that would more than cover all pilfered ice cream and an enormous tip.

"Did it not occur to you to ask the young lord to stop what he was doing?"

"Well, that wouldn't have been right, would it? Sending an

unlucky lot of children who hadn't gotten there quickly enough home without ice cream?"

"What about the store? What the young lord did constitutes theft."

The Prince sighed and looked at me, with a bit of pity I didn't like. "What the young lord did constitutes youth. You were young once, weren't you, Mr. Otxoa?"

And then I was bothered for a third time—not because the Prince insisted, as usual, upon ribbing me about this. But because his implication that I had lost all sense of fun hit too close to home. On this notion, the Prince was right. We settled into a silence then, my mind's energy split between wondering why I had denied myself the chocolate/vanilla swirl soft serve I had quite wanted and trying not to fixate on the way his lips pulled custard onto his tongue as he ate.

We wended our way back toward South Dulibre, traveling country roads from town to town in far more silence than that which had descended upon us when first we came. By the time my mind had shifted from my failings as a person to my failings as a civil servant and what I might tell the Queen of our first test, my own familiar energy swelled in my chest, the kind that only arose when trouble was near. Before I could register what imminent danger commanded my attention and whether the Prince was safe, I heard the shattering of the first pane of glass.

CHAPTER NINE

Xabier

"No matter what, stay here," Zain warned.

He had parked us crookedly on the edge of the town square, crossing traffic so that we faced the wrong way and the car was halfway up on the curb. Zain had identified the source of the ruckus far sooner than I had spotted the man—a round, middle-aged gentleman who I didn't recognize perched on a high branch in a tree.

Ignoring Zain's instructions completely, I exited the car with no real purpose other than to get a closer look and to begin to comprehend what was going on. Looking around the square confirmed the veracity of what we had heard. The glass of several storefronts of the shops on the square had been summarily shattered. From the looks of it, the cake shop had been hit, as well as the stationery store, a tailor and a dress shop. Scores of townspeople who ought to have been picnicking in the park square or enjoying a stroll in the shops cowered on side streets, as far away as possible from glass.

There was only one explanation. The man perched in the tree was a supo, and he had the idea to destroy the square. This was a job for the Ministry of Powers. Only, I was the minister and I felt utterly helpless to take action. Shouldn't help be on the way? I appreciated that Zain knew what to do, but I didn't like the idea of him in danger.

I winced at the jarring sound of yet more broken glass. This wasn't as heavy as the glass that had fallen from frames within wide storefronts—this glass came from smaller panes. My eyes scanned for its source and I was dogged to see that it had come off of the stained-glass windows of an adorable little chapel aligned center to the south end of the square.

What depraved mind possessed the will to sully a house of the gods? I watched on in horror, waiting to see what terrible destruction he might perform next. His target and purpose remained unclear. The oddly shaped panes of glass vibrated inside their frames a second before the glass itself burst.

He's using sound.

An unknown voice inside myself revealed to me the source of his power. I could not comprehend how I knew. Yet, I was certain that stopping the sound would stop the destruction. The palms of my hands tingled and itched and familiar warmth spread to my fingertips, much as they did when I was set to sweeten grapes. They wanted to do something, but what?

Distraction from the strange thoughts in my own mind were swept away as I returned to the moment, noting with alarm that I now stood even more alone. Zain walked toward the man, a crooked path through patches of ground that had not yet been spattered with glass. To do exactly what, I did not know.

"Hey!" Zain shouted loudly, cupping his hands around his mouth as one did when one wanted to throw one's voice, an attempt to get the man's attention. The stranger only continued to stare on, eyes moving sorrowfully around the square as fresh tears streaked his face. He was clearly aggrieved and some part of me thought to pity the him, yet unfamiliar sensations riddled my body.

No, not unfamiliar, the voice that had spoken to me earlier said. What came over me now was new, but it also felt quite right. Only, I couldn't identify precisely the purpose and nature of these feelings. The danger of the moment caused a natural reaction, but this didn't feel like adrenaline. It was some sort of energetic shift.

"Hey, you!" Zain shouted once more, his voice still failing to capture the man's attention. To my utter horror, Zain crouched to the ground and picked up a small rock, then hurled it toward the man with precision. What on earth was Zain Otxoa doing? The man was a faultless rule follower, and a keeper of the peace. Surely, throwing rocks at perpetrators wasn't part of his code.

Apart from that, I was fairly certain that assault by rock was against the law. I could admit to not having read the manual nearly as carefully as perhaps I should have done, but this seemed impermissible, even for an incident in progress.

The rock hit its target, which caused the man to scan the ground for the source of his attack. He set his gaze on me, then darted it to Zain. It all happened in the briefest of seconds, but, where he looked next, his eyes remained fixed. There was a streetlight with glass casing directly above Zain's head.

A fear that I had never known gripped me as I saw what was about to unfold. The man would shatter the glass of the lamp and broken shards would rain down on Zain, cutting him for certain, and possibly maiming him for life. In a split second, I thought not only of the lamp glass but of the glass of the bulbs themselves. Was it quicksilver in fluorescents? Whatever their inner workings, being hit by lighting components could bring nothing good.

No!

My only thought at that moment was to move Zain out of

danger. Only, my body didn't want to move. Why could I not command myself to lurch forward, to run fast enough toward where he stood to push him away? I kept my gaze focused on the tearful man, frowning deeply as my face and my hands heated with what I could only assume was rage.

No! I screamed again in my mind, willing him to stop.

Then, something different. The expression on his face changed. He blinked, as if in surprise. I darted my eyes again to the streetlight where his eyes had been trained. The glass remained intact. A glance back at the man, who seemed less sad in the moment than he seemed enraged, found him glaring down at Zain.

"Stop this destruction." Zain spoke the words in a voice that I didn't think I'd ever heard. And just like that, the man's brow unfurrowed, and every shred of sorrow and determination melted off of his face. I waited, breathless, for something more —for the man to set his sights on yet another thing to destroy. But his gaze remained fixed on Zain's face and he did no such thing.

∼

"You have powers," I whispered, my gaze still trained upon the remnants of what I had just seen. Even to my own ears, my voice rang with betrayal. Zain had just bent a man with terrifying power to his will with three calm words. My breaths were still shallow and my muscles begged me to move—to act out my surprise some physical way. I waited until the last of the other officers had walked away, when I turned my narrowed eyes to him.

A car had finally arrived from the Ministry, staffed with the officers who were meant to be assigned to the case. Zain and I showing up when we did was a simple stroke of luck. Not a full minute after Zain had spoken his magic had sirens from a distance begun to fade in. Zain had made quick work of directing the officers to identify and detain the man and he promised to file a report later, leaving the two of us, once more, alone.

"You have powers." This time my voice was stronger, less a question than an accusation, less uttered in shock than in disdain. "You are a royal."

It was the only logical conclusion. Half-bloods sometimes had powers, but they tended to be weak, as if the very fact of having diluted magical blood delivered trivial gifts. But nothing about Zain's power was diluted. What I had just witnessed was without a doubt one of the most impressive feats that I had ever seen.

"Please. Not here." His gaze darted between me and the car. "What I can tell you should not be spoken within range of listening ears or within sight of prying eyes."

Back in the car, I did not push. It still smelled faintly sweet, just like ice cream, but all the fun from earlier had been killed in one fell swoop. It didn't escape my notice that Zain looked mildly unwell. The notion that his body needed time to return to normal after such a display merely proved my theory. We rode silently back to the Ministry, rode silently in the elevator up to my floor, walked silently past Eusebio in a manner that must have spoken its own warning. The moment that Zain and I had stepped completely into my office, Eusebio silently closed the door.

"I suppose I should thank you."

Somewhere in the car, I had remembered my manners, though it would be wrong to say that I had cooled down. I remained jarred and unhinged by the day's developments. Skipping my desk in favor of my lit fireplace, I picked up my wine key and opened a bottle of Ichor, poured two glasses and held one out to Zain.

"I was only performing my duty." Zain took the glass with a shaky hand but did not drink. "I took an oath."

"But what do your duties entail? Tell me plainly. Are you a royal?"

"It's a bit more complicated than that."

I didn't like that I couldn't identify his emotion. His voice was the perfect mix of self-righteousness, bitterness and regret, with a bit of common deference sprinkled in for good measure. More so than usual, it sliced.

"I command you to explain in no uncertain terms." I surprised myself with my own forcefulness.

"You command me," Zain repeated, a clearer emotion beginning to form. He did not appreciate my phrasing. He spoke through gritted teeth and his eyes had gone dark as coal.

I hadn't commanded anybody to do anything since I was six years old. I'd gotten a handy scolding from my mother about how to talk to servants. But Zain wasn't my servant and I wasn't a child. I was a man who, by virtue of my position, would be deceived and mislead as a matter of course. So why did not knowing this about Zain hurt?

"I ask you to explain," I corrected. The fight had gone out of my voice and I kicked back to what I was feeling. "And I do thank you for salvaging the situation. But, please. I don't understand."

He looked off to the side and shook his head, looking entirely conflicted, as if he couldn't decide whether I ought to be allowed to know. Only, I already knew enough, so what was he holding back?

"You told him what to do, and he did it." I took a step closer, beseeching him. "That power is nothing short of brilliant. I've never witnessed anything like it—the power of control."

"It's not control. It's hypnosis," he said finally in a voice that had lost its bite. "My power is to encourage a specific action at the precise moment of consideration."

"Hypnosis..." I thought back to exactly how the events in the park had unfolded. Zain had spoken words and the sad man had done exactly what he'd said. There had been no pendulums or spoons stirring in teacups or dulcet voices telling anybody they were getting sleepy. Surely some elements of true hypnosis must work the same way they did on TV.

"Suggestibility is another way to say it. I suggest that something should happen, and my power persuades the person under my influence to make it so. I can't control what a person does, but I can lead them toward a certain decision. It doesn't feel to them like control. It feels like they've decided something for themselves."

I was still wrapping my head around all of it when a sudden, terrifying, infuriating thought occurred. The ground I had gained from taking a step toward him was erased as I took two steps back. Hypnosis as Zain's power explained everything. It explained the fog that liked to settle into my brain every time he was near. It explained why something caught inside of me every time he looked in my eyes. It told me why some part of me always felt out of control whenever he was in my presence. Perhaps everyone he did it to felt this way—some unidentifiable instinct that Zain Otxoa had them in his thrall. His sexiness only added to the effect. The most vicious predators were distractingly beautiful. It was all part of the disguise.

"You've been hypnotizing me," I accused in a low growl. "That's how you've kept me in line. That's how you've kept yourself safe."

A doubly panicked thought occurred then. If Zain truly held the power of hypnosis, he held the power to wash my mind clean. He had every incentive to make sure I did not remember anything he chose to reveal. For all I knew, these same truths had been revealed to me before and Zain had simply erased the memories.

"Are you daft?" he nearly shouted, quite insolently, I

thought. "If I were permitted to use my power to persuade you, don't you think that I would make things easier on myself? Or perhaps you think I enjoy petty skirmishes and hour after hour locking horns. I can assure you, *Your Grace*, that were I to use my powers to persuade you, matters would not be as they are."

"Then why—" I cut myself off.

"Why what?" He was still incensed. I had almost asked a question I was bound to regret. I couldn't argue with his logic, which caused me to conclude that he was telling the truth, which left me to my own alarming thoughts about brain fog and tight pants that I could not blame on sorcery. The short-lived theory was one I had been eager to espouse. It was a handy excuse for why I allowed him to speak to me the way he did and for how I chose to react. The truth was inescapable now: the way we were together was simple and unique to us.

"What do you mean, permitted?" I grilled, defaulting to misdirection. I was surely not planning to tell him all of that.

He rolled his eyes in exasperation. "Have you even read the manual? Section 6, Article 3, Page 20. *Should any person possessing powers of control, persuasion or influence be discovered, the use of said powers must be disclosed immediately upon discovery and be used at the sole discretion of the Queen. Furthermore, the possessor of said power is strictly prohibited from using the corresponding power to influence any royal, particularly those who hold the highest power and who sit on—or stand in succession to—the throne.* "

I blinked. "So even if you wanted to, you couldn't use it on me?"

"People with powers like mine aren't supposed to use them on anyone. Once we register them, we are sworn to secrecy. Centuries ago, those with powers like mine were sequestered and locked up—sometimes even killed. The ability to influence other peoples' powers are considered to be the most dangerous in the kingdom."

"Yet you just used your power without fear of retribution. Is it because you mean to make me forget what's gone on? Clean up my mind until no one is the wiser?"

I expected another eye roll at the accusation. Something inside me smarted when he simply looked sad. I supposed he didn't deserve this sort of interrogation over a power he hadn't asked for. Now, he simply looked tired when he answered.

"I already told you how the power works. I can't change what's in people's minds. I can plant the seed of a decision I want them to make, and then I can give them a nudge."

"You could suggest that I should forget it."

He shook his head. "Won't work. Deciding to forget something doesn't mean you will. If I influenced you to try to forget it, you wouldn't be able to and it would drive you mad. Making people forget things is a separate power. I've seen it before and it does fall under the mind control clause. But it simply isn't a power I have."

I thought about this for a minute. His logic still made sense. And I had to take into account what I knew about him. Zain Otxoa followed rules. It only led to one conclusion: everything I had seen him do just then had been sanctioned. His power was under the direct supervision of my Aunt Maialen.

"You are not who you say you are, in more ways than one," I mused aloud and studied his face. "The only role that makes sense for you is as an adjudicator. Yet, you masquerade as the Head of Internal Affairs, a job you dislike. But the more pressing question is, given all your competing duties, why have you so preoccupied yourself with me?"

"Perhaps you ought to ask the Queen."

CHAPTER TEN

Zain

I managed to make it back to my office before breaking down, though, during my clipped walk down the marble hallway, I had broken out into a cold sweat. Too out of sorts to use the elevator. I ducked behind a tapestry that opened to a secret corridor at the end of the marble hall.

The spiral of the hidden staircase only added to the sense that everything was spinning. I followed it three stories down, regretting most choices I had made that day all the while. I never should have brought Prince Xabier. I shouldn't have been hellbent on proving my point. I should have stopped it from getting so far. I never should have placed myself in a position to betray the confidence of the Queen. She was a fair ruler, but an order was an order. No matter how horrifically I was imploding, she would have to be my first call.

Right after I vomit.

I was relieved to arrive back to my own floor. The staircase was making me dizzy and I needed no more to add to these feelings of malaise. Actual illness could be cured with medicines, but nothing could soothe my worry. I slipped into my office through the secret door. Striding as quickly as my legs would carry me to my desk, I picked up the line and dialed the number. I wanted the Queen to hear the news from me first.

"Your Majesty."

The operators put me through when I used our code phrase for this circumstance: saying I was calling with a resolution over an earlier incident was code for an information breach.

"Mr. Otxoa. I am alone and the line that I am using is secure."

"I was forced to use my powers to de-escalate an incident with potential for Level 5 destruction. The Duke of Brix was present and witnessed my pursuit. He confronted me with his suspicions of my involvement and guessed correctly."

"Did you confirm or deny his suspicions?"

"I confirmed my involvement, Majesty and I shared with him the nature of my power. But I admitted that I was not at liberty to share broader context or other elements of the truth."

"What was his temperament as he discovered your true nature?"

"I believe the Duke was angered."

"He does not do well with betrayal. Or surprises of any sort," the Queen murmured under her breath. "Tell me—how did he surmise what you were doing? Was your persuasion so obvious?"

"I did not believe so at the time, my queen. No other bystander appeared to find the change in behavior of the perpetrator to be odd. Regardless, the incident is clearly a result of my sloppiness. I apologize. I recognize how this compromises your intentions and I see clearly how I have failed to perform my duty. I am at your service to do whatever you see fit."

"You're calling from your office at the Ministry."

"Yes, Madam."

"And the Duke of Brix? He is there?"

"As of a few minutes ago, yes."

"Ensure that the Duke does not leave the building and await my arrival. Your instructions are to stay."

After hanging up the phone with the Queen, I stared ruefully at my tumbler of wine, which I had been eyeing jealously since the moment I walked in. I could not take drink if I were about to meet with the Queen. It was all just as well given how out of sorts I still was. The sick feeling I had wouldn't likely be helped by imbibing too much.

But his eyes...

Thoughts of the sapphire blue of his irises cut through my thoughts. They always sparkled like jewels. Only, back there, they had dulled with something that looked like hurt. And it had come at the strangest of moments. It was one thing for his eyes to blaze with angry fire at not being told. But when he'd asked whether I'd ever hypnotized him, he had looked upset.

And then there was the other thought, a thought that should have had me rejoicing—there was evidence that the Queen's hunch about the Prince's powers was correct. I had felt it down to the marrow of my bones—the Prince had used his true powers to stop the streetlight from shattering over my head. The question that haunted me was *why?*

Why had his instinct to intervene failed to kick in for the entire day beforehand, when I had done everything in my power to ensure that it did? Had the instinct I had done everything to evoke revealed itself only when there was heightened danger? Was that how it worked? Or did it operate on some sort of odd delay?

Now that he had used said power, was it fully unleashed? Was he aware of what he had done? Or would the further use of his power involve drawing out more still? And a niggling feeling—a haunting feeling that I couldn't justify with rhyme or reason—was it a coincidence that the exact moment when he had chosen to utilize his power involved saving me?

CHAPTER ELEVEN

Xabier

"The first thing that must be said," the Queen began, "is that Mr. Otxoa has done a great service to his country. And that much of the trouble he's given you has been at my behest. He has taught you the work of the Ministry, eased you into an understanding of the true dangers that face us. He has groomed you to be able to face what is to come. Most importantly, he has monitored you, and been an assessor of your readiness, just as he was charged—by me—to do."

I looked between him and my aunt, disbelieving. "Groomed me," I repeated. "Assessed me? Assessed me for what?"

"To come into your true power, my child. Could you have truly thought that a royal of your superior lineage would be destined to make wine?"

She said it with such humor and the day had already been so jarring that I could not stop the faint tremble and the pout of my bottom lip when I answered. "Wine is the nectar of the gods."

"Indeed, it is," she conceded a bit more kindly, reaching out to pat my hand. "And you've done well with your Ichor."

This, she said with an eyebrow raise and a hint of accusation. She had known all along.

"Forgive me, Your Majesty. I meant only to honor South Abarra by producing award-winning wine. It was admittedly vain, but I could not bear another year losing the prize to the north."

"Which is exactly why I allowed it to continue. But it is the last deception from you that I will accept. We are in quite serious territory now." Her voice took on a different tone. "And it has come time for you to know the truth."

"What of my true power, aunt?" My heartbeat thundered and I felt ready to spin into a panic. "If I am not the Duke of Brix, who am I?"

"We bestowed you the title of the Duke of Brix—a title that you will keep—to convince you and all others that your powers are mild. Yet, nothing could be further from the truth. Your powers are so great that they had to be guarded, especially from the world but also from yourself. You are in possession of a devastating power, my child."

"But I turn up the sugar in grapes. I ripen them to make better wine," I practically whimpered.

"That's only half-right," Zain finally cut in. "The first half, to be specific. Your powers extend much farther than turning up the sugar. You can turn up all manner of things."

The Queen nodded in confirmation, looking positively conspiratorial. "And far more importantly than turning things up is your ability to turn things down."

I zoned out of my own mind for I didn't know how long. I thought about this—hard. It was difficult to confirm the veracity of a power I didn't think I had ever used. But why would I? Most things didn't need turning up or turning down, and the things that did had knobs and remote controls.

"I'm sorry..." I shook my head. "But, apart from making wine and giving your dinner a bit more salt, how is this remotely useful? Let alone devastating?" I could barely spit out the word.

"Just look around you. I see at least five things you could turn up to make devastating, right here in this room. The fire, for one." Zain jutted his chin. "Decide to turn that up and you'll burn down the whole building." Next, he jutted his chin to the thermostat. "Turn that down and you'll freeze us out." He strode to the drink trolley and picked up one of the two glass soda siphons on the bar set. "Turn up the quinine in this tonic water and you've got poison."

"The powers that sound the vaguest are always the most dangerous," Queen Maialen cut in. "Part of the work of the Ministry is to conceal the true nature of powers that could be misused."

"My queen, I see that you have confidence in me, but I am doubtful of my ability." I waved my hand toward the fire, and the drink cart and the dial on the wall. "I don't know how to do any of those things. When I'm around everyday objects, I don't get the feeling that I do whenever I'm in a vineyard. The grapes call when I walk among the vines."

"Just as your true power was concealed from you, your connection to your power has been muted by design. It wouldn't do for you to have an awareness of those powers before you were ready."

I stewed over this for another long minute with too many questions to ask. I chose but one. "Why now?"

Queen Maialen's voice was calm and even as she explained. "Because we don't have time to wait for your second coming of age."

But with each new answer only came more questions. I hated everything about this feeling. I couldn't think of a time when I had felt so naïve. And not merely naive—betrayed. Had my parents known anything about this? If Zain Otxoa knew, who else did?

"I had my first coming of age when I was twelve. I wasn't aware there was a second."

"We don't publicize it," Zain said in a voice that wasn't entirely unkind. His eyes were soft with something akin to pity. It made me pity myself. It didn't seem beyond the realm of possibility that I might cry.

"Most devos have a second coming," Zain continued helpfully. "*Devo* is our shorthand for those with devastating skill. Our best guess is that nature herself knows better than to unleash capabilities before a man is ready."

"Yet I am not ready." My gaze shifted from Zain back to Queen Maialen.

"Then we must ready you for your true duty, my child. Our nation cannot wait."

With that, the Queen rose, and I followed, though I felt wobbly on my feet. As I trailed her toward the door, I remained at a loss for words. I had raised every concern, voiced every doubt, made every true and persuasive point in the name of making it clear that I couldn't do whatever it was that was being asked. I still didn't know what this-all was for or what she expected me to do after she finally left.

"I know you have questions," she said finally as she stopped just inside the door. "Know that, by placing you in Mr. Otxoa's care, I have entrusted you with the very best. His talent for grooming those like you is legendary. He has been assigned to you exclusively these last years and will see you through your training. He has worked with the most powerful royals throughout the land."

My eyes flew to Zain, who—unnervingly—seemed only to study me for a reaction. My aunt patted me on the arm, bringing my attention back to her, before she proclaimed. "Tomorrow, Mr. Otxoa will help you begin the final phase."

An hour and three-quarters of a bottle of Claret later, I stood in my darkened living room, looking over the wretched, lit-up city and feeling sorry for myself. I wished my father here to answer for some of this, but had he ever really been? I wished my mother here to guide me, as she would have when she were alive. Only, she hadn't, which added to my bitterness. It was the first time I had ever not enjoyed a bottle of my delicious wine.

Is all of that over now?

It seemed that all my logical arguments for abandoning my post were moot and that I wouldn't achieve said goal at all. The very truth of things had thoroughly dashed my hopes. Worse, I had actively schemed for a different outcome. What I would now tell Fesik and Prince Oleander was beyond me. Just one day earlier, I had lamented the lack of eventfulness in my boring life. What a difference a day made. Jarring? Yes. But is the feeling I got when I worked among the vines something that I would trade?

A chime that I barely recognized broke me out of my thoughts. It wasn't common for my guards to summon me at this hour. On the strangest day of my life, I would not be surprised had there been more havoc. After all, I'd watched a middle-aged man sit in a tree and unwittingly stopped him from breaking glass.

"Mr. Otxoa is here to see you, Your Grace. Shall we let him up?"

"Yes," I said simply, then cut off the line. I briefly considered dressing, but I was in too odd a state of mind. It wasn't as if I had anything to hide. The man knew everything there was to know about me. He knew more about me than I even knew about myself.

In socked feet, pajama pants and a sleeveless white undershirt, I padded toward the door. The private elevator to the penthouse took no time to arrive.

I should not have been surprised to find the version of Zain

Otxoa standing in front of me to be quite transformed. For the first time ever, he wore something other than a button-down shirt and tailored slacks. For the very first time, there was no pencil tucked behind his ear. He looked real and different and beautiful, even in his exhaustion. He smelled like he always did. And, for reasons that I couldn't fathom, he looked sad.

"What's happened now?" I asked a bit snidely. "More news of not being who I thought I was? Let me guess—my true family is a pack of wolves."

I regretted it the moment the words flew forth from my lips. It only made him look sadder.

"Never mind," he said. "I shouldn't have come."

"Zain." I called, stepping through my doorway and bringing my hand to his shoulder to stop him from walking away.

He looked back in alarm, first at my hand on his shoulder and then back at my face.

"Please. Don't go. I'm being an ass and taking it out on you. When the truth is, you were only following orders."

I let my hand fall from his shoulder, wildly curious about the purpose of his visit. His intention to leave meant that he wasn't there in any official capacity. And not once since I had started working for the Ministry had he called on me at home.

"That's the first time you've ever called me that."

I swallowed around a question I felt sick to ask. "Is that even your real name?"

I might have been offended by the way his eyes laughed at me for asking the question. The truth was, I was relieved to see the hint of a smile. It didn't hit me until then that I was afraid, because however odd my strange exchanges with Zain, they had felt like ours. Now, the man who had provided the structure that defined my day-to-day had told me that everything was a ruse, which meant, by association, that things between us were a lie.

"Yes. Zain Otxoa is my born name."

"Born to who?" I wanted to know. He still hadn't answered my questions about the nature of his powers. In lieu of revealing more about himself, he'd instructed me to ask the Queen for explanation, which led me deeper into who I was myself, but which left plenty of unanswered questions about him.

"Arroa and Arestuz Otxoa, a master craftsman and a farmer, a son and a daughter of the same."

"And their parentage?" I pressed in a way I hoped wasn't altogether rude. But the not-knowing was awkward, at least as awkward as carrying on an interrogation in the threshold between the hallway and my home.

"I am not a halfling," he explained. "I'm something different. Something far more rare."

"Well, then, Zain Otxoa, rarest treasure of the south, do come in."

After I invited him inside and closed the door after him, I took him in from behind, noting that he looked at least as tasty in casual clothing as he did in his work attire. He wore tailored shorts and a dark linen hooded shirt with drawstrings that made me wish the both of us away to a breezy day at sunset on the beach.

"This is the first time I've seen you without your pencil," I remarked and resisted the urge to ask him whether it was part of the costume.

"It'll be odd to be out of the office," he replied. "You will be elsewhere these next weeks."

"I thought you were meant to train me." I frowned at the notion that something in the plan had gone wrong. Would I alone be out of the office, or would both of us go off someplace? "The Queen has said that you are the best."

"That's why I'm here."

The way he said it caused my heart to thunder.

"This part is never easy—the deception, the betrayal. I don't want to start things off on the wrong foot. I came here to see whether we couldn't clear the air. The person I've been as I was ordered to groom you for this—not all of it is who I am. I know you hate me. I was hoping we might start fresh. It'll be harder if things between us are unresolved."

Things between us.

I rolled the words over in my mind. Was there an us? There had to be. Or else he wouldn't be here. Or, maybe clearing the air was just something that he did with all the other devos who he had trained. I wondered how many there had been.

"I don't hate you," I admitted, a confession that hurt for how little I had done to prove otherwise. "I thought *you* hated *me*."

Zain blinked and frowned in surprise. "Why would I hate you?"

"Maybe not hate me. Just saw me for who I was: Inadequate. Disappointing. Unseeing of the value of anything you ever tried to teach me. I was a terrible pupil, yet you persisted in trying."

Zain shook his head. His hands were in his pockets. He looked younger in these clothes and it occurred to me I didn't know how old he was. Slightly younger than me, I had guessed. I had always longed to know more about him, and now that I knew who he wasn't, I was desperate to know who he was.

"Not that you apologized," he began. "But if you were to have offered one, there would have been nothing to apologize for. I was an intolerable twat."

He gave a little smile and a familiar feeling welled inside me—the one that came forth when we dropped the adversarial vibe. I rather preferred us as friends.

"So, what now?" I asked.

"Now, we move forward and forget everything that was bad about before—everything that made us less than who we truly are. We start over, even if only for a few more weeks."

With that, Zain started back toward the door. I wanted him

to stay. I wanted for him to drink with me and tell me more. But I was still too raw to ask for any of that.

"One more thing," I offered instead. "Since it's abundantly clear you know more about me than I know about myself, I think it's time you started calling me Xabier."

PART III

THE TRUTH

CHAPTER TWELVE

Zain

"Zain Otxoa arrives empty-handed?"

Xabier was in good spirits when I strode into his office the next morning, looking only slightly rough around the edges for someone who had been worse for wear. He was dressed as deliciously as ever in gray slacks and a light blue button down, but the slightest hint of dark circles under his eyes was a bit of a giveaway. His voice was deeper than usual. And rough.

"One of the many benefits of your training. No signing approvals for the foreseeable future." I replied. I mustered lightness to match his tone, a necessary attempt to set aside how it had been in his house the night before. For all the states that I'd seen him in, I'd never seen him drunk. My hubris that I knew him well from seeing him every day had clearly been an illusion. In all our two years working together, he'd never allowed his eyes to linger on me as they had the night before.

He smirked. "I was certain there would be more."

For once, he hadn't had his back to me when I'd walked into

the room. Eusebio had let me right in, seeming a bit bewildered to inform me that the Prince had been expecting me.

"You are temporarily relieved of your duties. Duke Oleander will cover your shift for the foreseeable future, but he won't know why."

Some of the humor on Xabier's face fell as he considered—for the first time, I was sure—that his scheme to install Duke Oleander would never be successful. At some point, he would have to be made aware of all this.

"What shall we do then?"

He had already been standing but he walked around to the front end of his desk, sat on the edge and extended his legs to cross his feet. There was a lightness about him that I could only guess owed to the freedom of vindication. He finally knew that the Queen had a grander plan.

Part of me felt lighter with relief from that burden. To feel better was why I had gone to him the night before, yet, when I awoke that morning, some part of me still felt sick. Known better by me than anyone, the second coming of the Prince's powers put my time with him solidly in the home stretch. This was the beginning of the end.

"Do you have your security badge?" I asked.

"My—" He cut himself off and shook his head. "I think they issued me one at some point, but ... everybody knows who I am."

"Where we're going now, security is high."

"This is one of the most secure buildings in all of Abarra." He repeated a line that we tended to repeat at the Ministry.

"Not if you don't even need your security badge to get in," I pointed out wisely. "And we're not staying in the main office building. We're going downstairs."

∽

"Fucking unbelievable," the Prince groused, taking in all his eyes could see with the wonder—and perhaps the terror—of a child in between the hippopotamus pool and the tiger cage at the zoo. "How is it that all of these people—and not I, the actual Minister—have clearance for this?"

We had taken one of the secret passageways to one of the secret elevators that led to the subterranean headquarters for all covert operations. The intervenors took up the majority of the facility.

"There's a training center due west, almost at the ocean. You'll go there, too, to hone your power."

Xabier spared me a glance. "Isn't that what we're doing right now?"

I shook my head as I let us into my real office—significantly posher than the MLM office I inhabited upstairs. It even had false windows made of high-definition screens that made it look as if palm trees blew in the wind outside and that my office was just a stone's throw from the beach.

"Right now, I will explain to you the whole truth of how all of it works." I motioned for him to sit. The Scandinavian style white sofa was nowhere as stylish as his, but it was a good place for him to settle; it was next to the whiteboard that I would use to lay things out.

He sat on the edge of the seat, body leaned forward, with his forearms propped on his knees, more eager in his attention than I had ever seen him. I felt twinges of excitement as well. This forbidden knowledge—the sheer brilliance of how the Ministry truly worked—was astounding, though it would never receive its due credit in the public.

Without further ado, I flipped over the whiteboard to the side where I had already mapped out how all of it was organized—color-coded, of course, in various markers.

"According to the public..." I dove right into a speech that I had given before. "The Ministry has the standard three divisions."

The Prince nodded and rattled off what both of us knew for good measure. "The Department of Registries indexes what power is held by whom when royals come of age and monitors abuses of power. The Training Division provides mandatory course work on the responsible use of abilities. The Protectorate works in conjunction with law enforcement to respond to calls and to adjudicate abuses of power."

"Yet there is a fourth division."

I motioned to my chart, which had one parent box up top that said "Ministry" and four child boxes below it that had the letters R, T, P and I.

"What does the I stand for?" the Prince asked, having already cited the R, the T and the P by way of his own explanation.

"The I stands for intervenors."

The Prince blinked in a way that told me I would have to spell it out for him, even though he had seen it all in action before. He had performed the role without even knowing what he had done.

"Intervenors *use* powers to *stop* powers. Think about it, Xabier. It makes all the sense in the world."

He frowned for a moment, as if scanning his mind for examples to prove or disprove this assertion. "Royals use powers to stop powers all the time. My own twin cousins—the Princesses of Arroa—are quite adept at this. Marjorie can make everything wet, and Markena makes everything dry. You haven't seen anything until you've seen them go head-to-head in a sandcastle competition."

"You said *royals*," I pointed out, dropping another breadcrumb that would lead him to the big prize. "Yet, few royals work for the Ministry. No matter how useful their powers, you don't see royals stepping forward to use them to keep the peace."

"Yet, intervenors keep the peace," the Prince said more than asked, following along on my logic.

"Yes." I nodded. "Indeed, we do. And very few intervenors are royal."

The Prince raised his eyebrows at my use of the word "we."

"You are an intervenor," he concluded.

"Among many other things." I wove my head back and forth. "But I am also not a half-blood. I—and the few others like me—am something quite rare. Royal blood does course through my veins, but my common blood did not leave it diluted. By contrast, it has left me a devo: one with devastating power."

The Prince narrowed his eyes. "But that is not the working of things."

I shook my head. "Not the working of things according to what we tell the public." I motioned to the facts and figures part of my whiteboard, which held a pie chart applicable to exactly this.

"Eighty-eight percent of the population is common. Seven percent is royal. It is widely acknowledged that some small percentage—let's call it five percent is half blood. It is also widely believed—even by half-bloods themselves—that to be partially royal is to possess diluted powers. It is known that half-bloods rarely register, and they are largely perceived not to be a threat."

"But your power is not diluted," the Prince followed.

I picked up a purple marker from the trough and drew over the half-blood section of my pie chart, changing the five of the five percent to a three. Then I wrote two percent next to a question mark and wrote the word "skilled."

"That's what they call people like me—those of us who are

certainly not of royal blood but who have powers that rival and best those of royals."

The Prince's jaw stayed slack and he sat back in his seat and ran a hand through his hair.

"So, what you're saying is that some commoners have powers?"

"It's a bit more complicated than that. Some DNA analysis has been done. Those like me hold one thing in common: smaller amounts of royal blood from every major line. The half-blood child of a king is likely to be born with weakened powers. But as half-bloods breed with half-bloods, power builds up the other side."

The Prince gave a hard blink and stared at me with wide eyes. "And you?"

"I'm what's known as one-sixteenth. Half-bloods up and down the line on both sides, from my parents, to their parents to their own. To the Queen's knowledge, I am the only one. But don't be fooled—those like me who are stacked even to the quarters or the eighths are quite powerful. For obvious reasons, those like me often choose to live under the radar. Some of us are called to serve."

Abruptly, the Prince stood. I had no notion of what he might do next. In my own experience, people dealt quite differently with shock. When his standing turned to pacing, I kept out of his way.

"But the protectorate cleans up incidents that have already happened. How do intervenors work if the system responds to calls?"

"You saw it in action, yesterday, with the man and the glass. If intervenors are on site, they can prevent incidents in progress from worsening. The intervention division has planted undercover agents to do just that, as first responders. We do high-risk work as well—attend events where shenanigans are likely to occur. Our predictive algorithm rates them all. Our intel on the likelihood that a supo will strike is impeccable."

At that moment, the Prince had been pacing away from me. He rounded on me suddenly, his face pained as he spoke the only sensible next question loudly and in a panic.

"Then why does the Ministry suck?"

My own reaction in that moment surprised me. Emotion welled inside and the prickle of tears rose to my nose and the backs of my eyes, too mild for the Prince to see, but I knew.

"Because we haven't had a talent like yours in more than one hundred years. Intervenors can only neutralize powers in the moment—no matter how powerful these skills might seem. Only a person of royal blood—and not all royals at that—have powers whose effects can be used over the long term."

The Prince didn't resume his pacing. I gave him time and watched in fascination as emotions I had never seen played over his face.

"I'm to use *my* powers to permanently subdue the powers of other royals?"

"Only the most dangerous ones, or repeat offenders that cause the costliest damage, and only with express approval of the Queen. With your power, we can cut Level 4 and Level 5 incidents by more than ninety percent."

His voice was full of disbelief. "And the Ministry will cease to be a laughingstock?"

"The Ministry—and you—will be revered." I took a step toward him, unable to stop my beaming grin. "You will be the best minister who ever was."

CHAPTER THIRTEEN

Xabier

"Sorry about the hood. Security and all."

Zain's first words as he greeted me at my chauffeured car were an apology. Security at Biarroa was something else. Designed to protect the identities of all involved—from the staff to the trainers to the devos themselves—hoods were to be worn at all times except in the cottages and when trainers and pupils were in the gyms.

"It does seem a bit extreme." I spoke after I tore off the offending garment, certain that my face was red and my hair tousled from having been confined to the impractical thing: a full-face balaclava that rather made everyone who wore it look like a thief.

I blinked thrice in rapid succession. My eyes were adjusting to the light. The tint on the car windows used on property was dark. Disoriented as I took in surroundings that required explanation, I felt vulnerable. I didn't enjoy all of the secrecy—my fazed awakening to the notion that I no longer held carte blanche to a world I had always been told belonged to me.

"There are reasons," Zain began. "Anyone who knows too

much could be a target for kidnapping, or blackmail, or exploitation. Even worse, a turncoat could be a perpetrator of all three. The less that is known about who dwells here, the safer it is for all of us. Information is leverage. But it also means risk."

His words were gently delivered. My hands were on my hips and I listened with a nod.

"Tell me about this place," I commanded just as gently as he had spoken. "Not just this..." I motioned around the hangar. "All of Biarroa. I assume that I'm meant to know."

The training facility was 30km due east of Dulibre down an unmarked, unassuming and highly secured private road. After I had received a full tour of the underground facility back in Dulibre, Zain had told me to pack my bags.

"It's ten-thousand acres," Zain began. "Forty kilometers square. Sixty percent developed. Training gyms just like this have been built and spaced strategically throughout. When devos are learning to use their powers, accidents can happen."

"What of the other forty percent?"

"The terrain on the developed land is varied—part of a deliberate design. The intention was to test as wide a range as possible of powers. Thousands of acres of land on the far western side will eventually be customized to test powers unforeseen.

"Each training gym is a little bit different. The needs of each trainee differ as well. I won't be the one training you—Mathias will. For the next several weeks, you will work with him and a skilled team of others. This gym was built specifically for you."

I blinked once, my façade of calm readiness breaking. I uncrossed my arms and took a step farther inside. I had been the Minister of Power for more than two years. If Queen Maialen had appointed me with all of this in mind, plans for my training had been years in the making.

"Show me. What are these numbers?"

Zain turned with no small bit of pride to the main hangar floor. Stations marked one through four by long flags that hung from the ceiling took up each of the corners. The entryway was through wide sliding doors in the middle of the shorter end, which is where we stood. A wide walkway between stations one and two led to a circle in the middle of a crossroad that delineated stations three and four. Whereas a smattering of objects and testing stations were strewn across the floor space in stations one through four, the circle in the middle was painted in purple. Above it hung a flag of the same hue that displayed the number five.

"Your training will happen in five phases," Zain began to explain, walking us forward and to the left, where he motioned to the objects in station number one. "First, you will practice your power on inanimate objects. They are regarded as the easiest sort of thing to influence, as these things go. Though the objects represented here may seem random or commonplace, mastering each of them will be an important steppingstone to going to the next phase.

"Go ahead," he urged when I walked too gingerly. "Touch anything. It won't break."

I just shook my head, slightly and quickly, and stayed on the corridor side of the line, overwhelmed.

"From there," Zain continued, motioning across the corridor to station two, "you will move onto the elements—not as straightforward to work with, unfortunately."

The seemingly random purpose of the mismatched elements came together in my mind. Two fire pits—one air, one gas. A fan and a swamp cooler. A stone fountain. These were simple things that could be done inside. I had seen natural features around the property that I might practice working with as well.

"For the third phase, you will work on living things," Zain

continued, speaking in a calm voice and strolling at an easy pace meant to disarm me.

This station looked more like a greenhouse, though it wasn't encased in glass. Grow lights were bright and hung above rows and rows of various flowers and plants. This part of the area was visible from many feet away.

"Given what I can already do with grapes—which seem to fall into the third category—shouldn't I be adept at the earlier two?" I asked.

"In theory, yes. It's possible that you are already proficient—that you have used your powers without knowing what you were doing." He hesitated. "You do know that you used them with the glass, in the park? The man meant to shatter the streetlight—the one above my head. He didn't, because of you."

The same kicked feeling that I'd had the day before punched into my chest—only, this time, it wasn't from betrayal. This was an altogether different brand of shock. The truth was, I *hadn't* known.

"All I remember was seeing his intention and wishing—" I cut myself off.

Zain's voice quieted. "Wishing what?"

For a moment, I considered denying it. But, in the spirit of coming clean... "I screamed at him in my mind not to hurt you."

My confession was met with silence. I couldn't put words to the emotion in Zain's eyes, but I had given something away. Without a doubt, I could see that he knew. Only, I had barely admitted it to myself and I don't know that I had ever planned to. I was overwhelmed and still sorting myself out.

"Whether your power comes easily or not," Zain finally got back on track, "the main goal of training is to practice. It's not enough to possess a power—you must learn to deliver it with surgical precision. Remember, animals are also living things."

The expression on my face fell as Zain spoke the words, at

the exact same moment when a small area with animals in cages revealed itself as part of the third space.

"We must be certain that your powers are extremely well-controlled before we move on to animals. If I've ever been hard on you, Xabier, the gravity of your power is why."

My eyes widened at his use of my given name and it did something to my insides when his lips softened into a slight smile.

"From you? I would not expect anything less."

"The fourth station," Zain continued, a bit flustered, "is for composites. The ability to alter one component of something but to allow the others to remain intact. It's like the example I gave you in your office that day—things like turning up the quinine content in tonic."

"What is that contraption?" I asked.

"It is a convection oven. You are fond of foreign bakery, are you not? At some point, we have it on the schedule for you to double the amount of chocolate chips in a batch of baked cookies."

I smiled once more, amused and a bit impressed.

"You've thought of everything, haven't you?"

Zain's expression became self-righteous. "Contrary to what some people believe about me, I like to have a bit of fun."

He held my gaze for longer than strictly necessary and I could not turn away. It caused me to think—once again—of the night before, of things said for the first time and things not said at all.

"And the fifth phase?" I asked finally, my eyes remaining on Zain rather than turning back toward the purple circle that we had already passed. Thoughts about the fifth phase may have been the only one that could have broken the spell. They rooted me back into the danger of all of this.

"During the fifth phase, you will master turning human powers up and down."

I half-blinked. "What if— "

I didn't need to finish.

"You will only attempt that ability if you have mastered the previous four phases, and only then if you are confident that you can be successful in your attempt. By that point, you will have a better sense of how well you can control your powers. We will know better about the wisdom of proceeding then."

I nodded lightly and finally broke his gaze, crossing my arms once more and looking toward the purple area in the middle of the room.

"The markings are significant," Zain went on. "And your practice will be done in this room, on a human subject. When you embark upon it, a circle of five of the most powerful devos will surround you. If your own powers spin out of control, their combined powers should be enough to contain it, and to stop and repair any damage that was done to your subject."

"Should be?" I repeated with alarm. "Have these safeguards ever failed?"

Zain regarded me gravely. "Yes."

I quieted then, letting it all sink in.

"What shall happen should I fail to master these skills?" I asked finally. "Queen Maialen said that others are carrying the work. But that they have become exhausted. What if those powers falter?"

Zain's answer was more neutral than I would have liked. "In order to protect the realm, we must work with whatever resources we have."

I squared my shoulders and nodded. "When will I meet my team?"

"Tomorrow morning you begin. Today is orientation. And rest."

Suddenly, I was desperately afraid that he would leave. If he wasn't to be my trainer, and we were no longer in the Ministry every day, I could not imagine his role.

"What role will you play?" I asked directly.

"That of a consultant," he replied. "I will oversee operations behind the scenes, help to answer your questions and serve as an ambassador between you and the training team. A bit of moral support thrown in as well. We will be sequestered in a private cottage where we may roam freely and be unmasked within that domain. On my downtime, I'll be closing things out."

He could have given no better answer to my question. If the world insisted on moving beneath me, I would see to it that many things changed.

"In that case," I replied. "Let me make you dinner."

CHAPTER FOURTEEN

Zain

"Bacalao a la Vizcaina would be a welcome dinner, I presume?"

We had just settled into what was called the Palace Cottage, an unexpectedly modern but accurately small home next to a flowing creek. It was on the easternmost edge of Biarroa, nestled into the hills. When a devo was being trained, it was customary for his team to stay as a pod in one of the sequestered houses: servants, guards and handlers like me.

Only, Xabier did not travel with servants. Biarroa had its own fleet of chauffeurs who stayed at some central location away from here. His guards were on shift and stayed on patrol at the periphery of the cottage lot, as ever out of sight. During these next few weeks as he underwent his training, the only inhabitants would be me and him.

"I'm sure anything you make will be fine."

"But you *like* Bacalao a la Vizcaina..." he prodded. "I understand you come from Muela del Dragón."

He mentioned this fact casually at the same moment as he

placed a glass in front of me and began to fill it with white wine.

"I am," I confirmed haltingly. He had never asked me about, well, anything about myself. "And I do like Bacalao a la Vizcaina. I haven't had it in ages."

Xabier poured a glass for himself. "The restaurants in Dulibre never get it right. The fish is never as fresh and the tomatoes in our markets are wrong."

"You sound like a connoisseur," I remarked. He was quite right about all of that. "But how will you get the better ingredients out here of all places?"

He smiled conspiratorially. "They've delivered my standard order. Every Wednesday, when I'm in Dulibre, they fly in the correct ingredients."

I had tried not to seem too curious the night before during the minutes I had spent in his apartment. Since leaving, I had gone over the details in my mind. It had been wide open, with furnishings alone separating one space from another. Unlike the classic feel of his office at the Ministry, with its teal blues and golds, his apartment had been sleek grays freshened up by bursts of bright green interior plants.

"You don't have people to cook for you?"

He corked the bottle and shrugged. "I do. But I prefer to cook for myself."

"Who taught you?" I was curious to know.

"Mostly the Food Network," he admitted. "Though, the Bacalao a la Vizcaina, I learned from a chef I met on the island."

I couldn't help but wonder whether the chef had been a mere teacher or more than that. Showing someone how to cook could be an intimate thing. Xabier had always seemed solitary, but also content. It unnerved me to know so much about him professionally—to be able to predict his every reaction to our work—and be utterly in the dark about his personal life.

"I miss it," I admitted, speaking of my little island. Muela del Dragón was small but uniquely beautiful. It was where my house was and where I had grown up. Like Xabier, I maintained an apartment in Dulibre only for work, but Muela del Dragón was home.

"It has the best swimming coves in all of Abarra, north or south. It's a place where I wish to find occasion to return."

"You need no occasion. You're a prince."

He threw me a mock-reproachful look. "*Somebody*'s kept me tied up at work."

"Your Grace—" I began.

"Xabier," he corrected and went on as if I'd never spoken. "Work has kept me from doing all sorts of things I like."

My response was as much for myself as it was for him. "All of that can change now."

We raised our glasses in silent toast and I had my first swallow. I didn't know what it was, but it was good. A glance at the bottle told me it was something Portuguese. I enjoyed the satisfied smile that spread across Xabier's lips after he drank his first sip of wine.

"You'll leave the Ministry quite transformed," I went on, wanting to think of anything other than how difficult his training period would be if I had to eat with him every night and try not to melt from his lazy smiles. "Within six months, you'll have halfway worked yourself out of a job," I prattled on, eager to say anything that would get me back into my right mind.

"Good," he came back at the tail end of another sip. "With that all tied up and settled, we no longer have a need to spend our time discussing work."

Wait, what?

"What will we talk about then?"

This time, when he had his third drink of wine his blue eyes never left mine. He smiled lazily again before he answered.

"Everything else."

~

Four days in, and long days of training had left the Prince rather energized. These sorts of things could go either way. The training was equal parts physical and psychological—a total departure from anyone's common routine. I had seen many a first-week trainee fall asleep over their dinner plates or collapse from exhaustion by noon.

But, Xabier... His reaction proved that Queen Maialen had been right. His training seemed overdue. After a few early bumps, he had taken fully to his powers. It had been a true thrill to see. Overseeing his training had given me license to watch.

By design, the cottage served as a retreat—a tranquil respite from the intensity of the training gym. It sat next to a creek with rushing waters that could be heard from the deck. One could relax in one of the hammocks by its banks or remain on the platform above, soaking in a heated infinity pool or the hot tub on its border.

We had taken to coming out to the pool at night. Dinner had proven insufficient to contain our conversations. Xabier had questions—dozens of questions—for me. I chalked it up to the sum of all that had changed. He was adjusting. Reorienting himself. Reinterpreting his world during a time when the ground moved beneath him. And I was part of his world—for the time being.

He will break your heart.

I couldn't help but think it in the moments in between, when neither one of us was speaking; in the moments when his glow was upon me; in the wickedness of his smirks and the deep rumble of his laugh. And increasingly, in the heat of his gaze, something that had always lingered between us was coming to the fore. This situation had given it space.

I had resolved earlier that day not to judge myself for falling for a handsome prince. It seemed practically a rule that one must. I was certain it would be the end of me but did not resist what could no longer be kept at bay. It explained why I had allowed myself to lie by the pool on the back deck of our cottage, feet bare and legs dangling into the water, as the Prince and I shared a bottle of after-dinner wine.

"So, are we, or aren't we?"

His voice was deep and his question was a non-sequitur. Minutes earlier, we had been discussing the stars. They shone brighter than they ever did in the city. Xabier had poured us one more glass of port and listened with quiet patience as I'd told him about a time in the States when I'd seen an epic meteor shower.

"Are we or aren't we what?" He got philosophical, the more he drank. This could be an existential question.

"I suppose that I am still the Minister of Powers. So, I guess what I'm wondering is, are you still my employee?"

It was too dark for him to see me make a sweeping motion with my arm, which is exactly what I did before proclaiming, "We all are."

"It poses some difficulty," the Prince remarked, "when the vast majority of the people I meet are subordinated to me in some way. It's one of the unadvertised benefits of being third in line to the throne. It makes forging friendships—and anything else—rather complicated."

Between the food and the wine, Xabier's suggestion sounded like one of the most preposterous things I had ever heard. I chuckled heartily.

"I am the thorniest thorn in your side. And you want to be friends?"

I thought it was hilarious, but I stifled my laughter when I could see he was beginning to look a bit offended.

"No, Mr. Otxoa. Not friends."

Oh.

Before I could react, he moved the bottle and the glasses, propped himself up on his elbow and rolled over on his left side, peering down at me and not looking intoxicated in the slightest. I wondered absently whether his power made it so that he couldn't get drunk, like starting off as some sort of wine god had made him immune. I was too buzzed to do the mental math, and defaulted to the conclusion that it didn't make much sense.

"You're beautiful," he whispered, and the way he said it, I knew he meant it deeply. "I've wanted to tell you before. And since I'm fairly certain you don't work for me anymore, I thought it might be time."

"I was only tricking you into thinking I worked for you. I was under the orders of Queen Maialen all along. Technically, she is my boss."

"Even better," he whispered. "Then I won't feel an ounce of creepy guilt for doing this."

He put his warm hand on my shoulder for the briefest of seconds before sliding it to my neck and palming the back of my head in his hand. He stroked the tip of my nose with his before capturing my lips in a kiss. I'd been told that they were luscious, which I had never fully understood or appreciated as a compliment until the moment that I tasted his.

His lips were soft but his kiss was hungry, slow but urgent all at once, deep and fixating, as if I couldn't pull away. It drew me out of myself and into myself and upside down and inside out, and with every passing instant, much closer to him.

We both made sounds, I thought. Only, I couldn't really think, and it could be that the muffled moans existed only in my mind. The blood flow in my brain could not have been adequate for as quickly as most of it had gone rushing to my groin. Kissing the Prince was sexy as hell.

"Zain," he whispered as he pulled away.

I had just had some sort of kiss-gasm. I knew that wasn't a thing. Only, kissing Xabier, it was—some sort of climax that came at the height of our epic kissing that left me intoxicated and sated and spent. We kissed once more—long and magnificent—then pulled away again to catch our breaths, then recovered quickly, ready to go right back in again.

Somehow, we went from being propped up on elbows to being propped up on hands to practically climbing into each other's laps as we kissed. I was only peripherally aware of this movement, which fully explained my utter surprise when we landed—fully clothed and clinging to one another—in the pool.

A splash of surprise. A bit of laughter. Ruined cell phones and wallets possibly, and, best of all, some very clingy, wet garments. We somehow resumed our kissing and half-walked, half swam to the shallow end all at once. In three feet of water, it was easier to kiss and touch and rub and to divest ourselves of our clothes.

"Fuck, you're sexy."

My first words in minutes were utterly unnecessary. The state of my cock said it all. In three feet of water, I was up to my thighs, my balls grazing the top of the water, with my cock, hot and ready in the night air. A cold pool of water was no match for a hot Xabi.

He backed me up to the low wall, pressing our bodies against each other once again as we kissed, our cocks colliding deliciously as we made our fumbling way. Once we got to the edge, he gave me the smallest of lifts to seat me fully on the side. From there, he stopped the kissing, bracing me with a strong arm holding my back as he looked down at me.

"So beautiful, Zain."

He bowed his forehead until his touched mine, and he closed his eyes. At that moment, he threaded the fingers of his free hand into mine and I wondered whether he was drunk after all. Only, I felt sober and everything he was doing felt real. He opened his eyes and they were so dark. Hard to see, but so complex. My dick throbbed against his stomach and he blinked, then ground against me, then let out a breathy growl I didn't think I would ever forget.

From there, he bowed me back, kissing down my jaw and my neck, and down my nipples and even lower still. He squatted in the water until he stood at exactly the perfect height. Only when his hands were on my thighs and his mouth was on my cock and my head was thrown back in ecstasy did I realize that I was completely in love with him.

CHAPTER FIFTEEN

Xabier

"Did you see me today?"

I called to Zain as soon as his form came into view. He appeared to be reading on the deck. I could hear the excitement in my voice as I pulled off my sweatshirt and tugged off my hood. I had run back to the cottage, metaphorically speaking, of course. It reminded me of my days as a schoolboy, tearing away from my lessons in order to rush through the fields to get to the secret fort. In this case, it was a little cottage by a stream that I had begun to think of as ours, the three weeks that we had spent here a blissful eternity. Instead of Fesik and the other boys, Zain awaited me to play.

"I thought I made you nervous."

It took a long moment for my gaze to reach his eyes, which regarded me with humor. I was too appreciative of his lithe form as he lounged on the chair. He sat in the shade of the afternoon, simply warming himself in the dry, gentle breeze, his smooth, luminous skin beckoning me to relieve him of his adorable, fitted, chartreuse swimming trunks.

"You do," I admitted. "But you have a habit of ignoring my requests and doing whatever you want in the end."

His magazine fell to his lap and he gave me a look. "Pot, meet kettle."

"Well, did you see me or not?"

"I only peeked in the morning," he admitted. "I spent the afternoon plotting a slow seduction." He put the magazine down on the side table and swung his legs around until he sat sideways on the lounger. "Why? What new trick did you learn?"

From there, I launched into the story of how I had mastered all of the composites in a single day—from liquids, to solids, to gas. I had turned ocean water to pure salt; turned a chamber of ambient air into 100% nitrogen, then given it its oxygen back; I had neutralized carbon dioxide—a feat the supervising scientist hadn't believed my ability could do. There was talk of what it all meant for the ozone layer.

Zain insisted that he was very impressed and lavished me with princely praise laid on so thick that we both had to chuckle. When he pouted with complaints of how sweaty I had been coming home these past days, the plan of his seduction became clear. It involved getting naked and rinsing off in the creek, then moving the party to the shower. Hours later, we were cuddled in the tub, eating honey and nuts and cheese with fingers that were pruny as all get-out. Every day when I left the training hangar, I was exhausted. That day, I had dozed on the short ride from the gym to the car. Yet, one look at Zain —one suggestive glance every time I came back—rejuvenated me.

"They've named a day for the final test," I told him after long moments of quiet, as we clung together and petted and lounged. In our days together at the cabin, we had shared so much more than sex.

"When will it be?"

His voice was neutral, and I lounged in his arms, which

meant that I could not see his face. The sun had long-since set. Perhaps he was lulling into sleep.

"Thursday," I said. "Five days from now. They need to call in all of the guardians who will be there to hold space."

"You have excelled at your training, Xabi. You must know at least that."

It had become evident that I had learned quickly. After the early, difficult days, I had sailed through tasks with increasing speed. The coaches had been careful what they said around me, so as not to build overconfidence. But I'd heard some of their chatter and seen some of the astonishment on their faces.

"What if I fail?"

My voice was so quiet that it could barely be heard above the stirring of the water, as wayward fingers and toes tickled the bubbles on top.

"You won't." He pressed a kiss to my temple. "And even if you do, you have mastered a set of skills that will still prove invaluable to the Ministry's work."

"Will you come be with me on that day? I know that I banned you, but ... I don't think I can do it without you."

He pressed another kiss onto my head.

"Of course I will be there. I will serve as one of your guardians."

I spited the instinct that told me to sit up, daring not to leave the sconce of his arms. "You will?" I blurted out with excitement.

"Remember only this: if your power has spun out of your control, seek me out with your eyes or turn to me when I call. I will tell you then exactly what to do."

∽

"REMEMBER. YOU'VE DONE THIS BEFORE."

Zain's final words to me were whispered as he crossed

through the purple circle to take his place. It measured twenty-five feet across. I followed him only briefly with my gaze before bringing my attention back to the others. There were two devos who I had just met, each with a different power, and Queen Maialen herself.

Along with Zain, this group would form the circle that served as my container. I did not want to hurt the poor man who would be my test subject—or worse. Zain's power of suggestion, paired with the ability of a devo called Demi who could create illusory diversions and that of another devo called Nico who could bend energetic fields until they broke, were intended to save the man if my power could not be controlled.

It took effort to drown out the voice that insisted on reminding me that I'd acted out of pure instinct that day—the one when I'd kept the man from shattering more glass. *Having* powers was one thing. *Harnessing* them was another. I would attempt to turn up or turn down the powers of my subject as the situation prescribed. But there were dangers—one misguided push and I could stop his heart.

"Your subject has arrived."

Mathias had been my head trainer, with me since day one. At first, I had been disappointed that my trainer wasn't Zain. He had seemed all knowing and had functioned as my coach all these months when he'd tolerated me at the Ministry. Then, Mathias had worked me and worked me harder still and I came to realize how much I preferred Zain as the person in whom I sought sanctuary. Nothing compared to the respite I found in his arms.

Sometimes, attraction is only that—a spark that crackles between two people, a flame fueled by a breath of air so fleeting that it quickly dies. Only, there was nothing fleeting about me and Zain. The spark had always been there. The lie had sucked the air out of the room. Then, the air of truth had turned us into a five-alarm blaze.

"Where is he?" I asked Mathias, who stood at the fifth spot within the circle. He was a human magnifying glass. He knew how to laser-focus light. Three weeks ago, it would have sounded to me like a mostly useless power. Only now did I comprehend the true wonder of so many abilities. The man could harness the power of the sun.

"In front of you, my child."

Queen Maialen spoke from where she stood and inclined her head toward the middle. It dawned on me at the same moment that a disembodied masculine voice came from precisely that spot.

"My power is invisibility."

My hands prickled, possibly with sweat. Either that, or my power was waking, knowing already what I needed to do. Fascinating aspects of my abilities had already begun to unfold. Whereas a golden glow seemed to shine on my hands when I worked my magic with clusters, I had since discovered that wielding my powers in different ways created different colored glows. With my earlier tests, I had learned to create the desired outcome by visualizing the result.

Only, now... how could I visualize the appearance of a man who I had never seen? How could I use my power to manifest a result I didn't understand? My powers spiraling out of control suddenly seemed the least of my worries. Even if I had been able to envision him, I was all turned around in my approach. Was I meant to turn visibility up or invisibility down?

It has to be the latter.

In the absence of knowing what he looked like, success would be a matter of diminishing his powers of invisibility so that his unknown figure would emerge. Through my training, I had discovered that my left hand dominated in matters of turning up. Conversely, my right hand dominated in matters of turning down, which meant I had to use my right hand in a manner that would not draw suspicion in public.

I approached the middle, having the benefit of the small delineated circle that let me know at least where the subject stood. As I approached, I could feel the subject's heat. I thought of how I would have to act in public to remedy this, if we were back in that town square that day with the man who was breaking glass. I got into character then. I was a jogger, out for a run. I jogged in place for a long few seconds to get the point across. My masquerade for using my power would be to stop and stretch.

And, from there, I tried. I tried to push my power out toward the invisible man using a technique that I had learned as I hid it in a side stretch, left hand on my hip as my right hand pushed it up toward where he stood. For the briefest of flashes, I saw the beginnings of a transparent hulk of a person. I was on the right track, but I needed more. I needed to find a way to push my power that didn't make me look like a sorcerer in a fantasy movie. That sort of thing would be way too obvious.

I tried a different stretch then: my right arm across my chest and a flexing of my palm which made me look natural as stretches went. It was a direct line between me and my subject and I could see it did a little better. This time, a flash of him appeared long enough for me to see that his back was to me and that he had dark, short-cropped hair. But I made a quick conclusion: something about the awkward angle of my arm across my chest was limiting the power that flowed.

I jogged in place once again, an attempt to keep my own energy moving and thought about my best approach. And then it came to me: I would do an overhead shoulder stretch—the kind where I could extend my arms with my palms out. The more I thought about it, the more I began to think this could create optimal energy flow.

I stepped back from the invisible man, took a deep breath, spread my feet shoulder-width and bent over into the stretch. I had learned that only I could see the glow of my own hands.

Even as I bent over, with energy flowing through my back and my shoulders, the glow of white was visible inside my peripheral vision.

Also in my peripheral vision, I could see the figure of the man emerge, gradually becoming solid in his opacity as my energy flowed. It wasn't easy and I was sweating, and it was an awful angle, but I was doing it. Nobody was shouting at me to stop and I heard no sounds of distress.

What I did begin to hear when the man started to look fully solid and fully formed were the sounds of the circle's applause. A moment came—as it always did—when I knew from instinct that it was time. I was laughing as I brought myself back to standing, seeking out Zain's proud eyes first. I finally turned toward my subject—walked around to see him. My smile disappeared out of sheer surprise.

"Eusebio?"

~

After I had seen off Aunt Maialen and basked a little beneath her praises, I went in search of Zain, who had retreated back to the cottage an hour before in his own car. He had stood back and allowed me my victorious moment—the pats on the back from the other guardians, from my trainer, and from the Queen herself.

I had seen my aunt to the airport. In the car, we had spoken in concrete terms about my role, how it would change, and how I would spend my time. Given my new powers, a new council would have to be formed for those with only the highest security clearance to determine how semi-permanent revocations of power would be decided. We discussed Zain's role. He would have to be consulted, of course. Given his experience, I could not imagine his absence from that council.

"Zain!" I called. Lights were on in nearly every room, which was why I couldn't tell where to look for him first. I had expected to be tired after my trial and after the sleepless night that had preceded it. But, at that moment, I felt vital.

"Zain!" I called a second time when I found him neither on the deck or in the kitchen. He wasn't in the living room or even the theater room watching TV. It wasn't like him to nap during the day, but I found him in the bedroom, not napping but still up to no good. To my utter horror, Zain was packing.

"Where are you going?" I demanded. It took only an instant for my spirits to turn around—an instant to go from elation to alarm.

"Your training is complete." His voice and his eyes were empty. He looked exhausted, as if something had erased all of the rest and down time he seemed to have enjoyed that week. Since he had participated as a guardian during my test, was he at some sort of energetic extreme? Had he overworked himself as part of an attempt to muster the strength to help me?

"You didn't answer my question. Where are you—" My voice stopped working and I couldn't get out the thought. Why wouldn't he look at me?

He stopped packing but didn't lift his gaze to meet mine.

"Home for a rest, at first. Then back to work, eventually. I need to just... I need to take some time."

"And then?" My voice shook because he had told me the answer, but I felt that I no longer knew. He had never lied to me since the night that the Queen had told me the truth. It made no sense that I wanted him to repeat it himself.

"And then I will do as I always do." He finally brought his gaze to mine. "I will finish my project and move on. I will be at the Queen's disposal to fulfill my duty."

"Whatever you thought this would be..." My wildly beating heart quickened my breathing. "Whatever you thought you would do when all of this finished... It doesn't have to hold. You've earned your right to anything you want next."

"I just want a rest."

"Then take it. But come back to figure it out—what you want with the Ministry, and what you want with me."

"I can have nothing with you." He smiled wryly. "As for the Ministry, I'll go where I am needed so long as it doesn't interfere with my ability to intervene from time to time."

I had a rational response to the second part, but I'd barely heard anything after the first.

I can have nothing with you.

"You can have nothing with me? According to whom?"

I didn't bother to try not to sound offended. In truth, I was deeply hurt.

"According to me. Xabier, you must know that it has to be over."

But I didn't know that. And I didn't expect or understand the hurt and the desperation and the resolve in his eyes as he spoke them.

"What if I needed you?"

I asked the only question that mattered.

"Trust me. You don't."

CHAPTER SIXTEEN

Zain

For the first time in ever, there was no joy to waking up in my own bed. The fact that Xabi had never visited this place did nothing to lessen the pain of his absence. In place of trying to explain how he felt missing in a place where he had never been, I got up. No lounging. No gazing out my windows, and certainly no lubricated fun. Morning wood had been murdered by my broken heart.

You don't get to play the victim, my inner critic scolded itself. It was true. I had been the one to do the breaking. But it was pre-emptive breaking—the kind you did to avoid the inevitability of being broken yourself. And it had been strategic breaking. I'd cut it off at a natural ending point. He had come to the end of his training. I had come to the end of a two-plus-year assignment—the biggest assignment of my career. I had earned my vacation and didn't have to be any place for at least six weeks.

That was just my scheduled time off—the time the Queen and I had agreed that I would take after this assignment ended. The truth was, I had years of banked vacation time. If I wanted to, I could be away from the Ministry for months. I could ask for a different job completely—ask that I not be reassigned.

Some part of me wanted to leave and never come back. Financially, I could afford to quit. The trouble was, I would wither away from not using my skill. Not moonlighting for two weeks as an intervenor had been a trial. And the piece I couldn't admit to myself yet was that I had to keep working at the Ministry. If I never went back there, I would never see him.

∼

TWO WEEKS HAD PASSED since I'd been at home. I'd given up on cooking—given up on everything, including myself. The only thing I was confident in anymore was my ability to wallow. Some of it was freshly needed wallowing. But part of it was pent-up wallowing, I had decided. Falling apart completely was the pendulum swing when you held yourself to my standards of service.

It was Saturday night. I should have been somewhere intervening. I wasn't, and I needed to fill the void. Fully committed to an evening plan of drinking my sorrows and eating my feelings, I wasn't surprised in the least when the doorbell rang. I had called in a delivery service to bring in the very best raw oysters. I would bathe them in mignonette sauce and—however un-festive I was feeling—would swallow them down with a fine champagne.

I hadn't gotten fully dressed, but I had put on my best silk robe, a forced display of whatever hope I had left. Bingeing on romantic Chinese dramas had given me the license I had needed to have a little cry. Having moved on to the stage of mourning that required reading O, The Oprah Magazine and actually taking its advice, I was poised to go out on a date with myself.

I swung open my heavy front door absentmindedly, simultaneously leaning over to the key table just inside. I knew what hell service staff endured and I enjoyed tipping. It was a habit I had picked up in the States during my studies abroad. Those had been exciting times. Perhaps I was overdue for a holiday that would take me back to my youth.

"Nice robe."

My gaze flew up at the sound of the voice that had haunted my every moment, to take in the face that had infiltrated my every thought. He held a heavy takeout bag in his hand—certainly mine, as the bag held a Styrofoam chilling chest. He must have intercepted the delivery driver or known somehow of my intentions. But I couldn't think about the "how." I had to think about the "what." My prince was here.

"I've been thinking about how you might look in blue and gold..." he trailed off, his eyes washing over my garment's design. Blue and gold were also the colors of his house.

"I think this belongs to you?" He held up the bag. I had yet to speak. More accurately, I could not speak. I took the proffered bag, motioned him inside and began padding toward my kitchen. I walked slowly in a vain attempt to collect myself. I scrambled for a notion of what to say. He looked bad—underslept and distraught—for reasons that I could fathom. Should I tell him how I missed him, and how beautiful he still looked to me?

Don't let him reel you in, commanded my inner voice of self-preservation. It convinced me that small talk wouldn't do. Chatting could lead to flirting, which could lead to kissing. Kissing would lead to something that would throw me down a hole I lacked the strength to escape from a second time. It would be safer to get to the point.

"Has something happened?" I thought to ask. It wasn't beyond the realm of possibility, though the Ministry had operated well for weeks without me.

"No, not at work." He had gotten my drift.

"Then why have you come?"

His soft, patient look wore at my resolve. "You know why."

"Let it go, Xabi."

"You must know that I won't do that. I've never made it easy on you when we didn't see eye-to-eye. If there's anything worth locking horns with you on, it's this."

When I replied, there was only sadness in my voice. "And I won't back down just because you like to win."

"This isn't about winning, Zain. This is about us."

"There is no us. We were an illusion—a deception born out of necessity."

"Are you certain? Because, for me, we were born the second we laid eyes on each other."

He took a step toward me. I was frozen to my spot.

"We were born again the first time we stood this close, and born again in quiet moments when I dared not voice what I was certain I was not worthy of. We were born again in our kisses and wrapped in the sheets of our lovemaking. We were born again a thousand times, Zain."

I closed my eyes against the ache. It had been weeks now since he'd begun to call me by name and still it gave me joy—the tiniest of gestures that renewed me somehow. It made me want to pull him inside and hide him away and keep him all to myself.

"You must trust me to know my own heart."

I saw his determination—his conviction in his own words. He was so convinced that his feelings were real, but I had to make him doubt himself. We were back where we had started—the Prince naïve but determined and me wise to knowledge that he did not possess.

"It's too soon to make big decisions," I argued. "They say after you've been through a big life change, you shouldn't do anything rash for at least a year."

The Prince did a full eye roll, which I didn't think I'd ever seen. If I hadn't been miserable, I might have laughed.

"I didn't just get out of rehab. We've got to stop you from watching so much TV."

"Xabi," I whispered, begging him now. "Please trust in my experience. You will feel differently—things will *be* different—in a couple of months."

"I won't make it a couple of months." His voice had quieted. "I've barely made it a couple of weeks."

We stood in silence then, perhaps at an impasse? I had lost all perspective. I didn't know whether I was wearing him down. But I was afraid that if he didn't leave soon, that I would ask him to stay. If I asked him, he would. And, if he did, I had no doubt that we would be together for months, or until he saw that I was right, and broke my heart to let me down.

"Do you not love me?" he whispered, as disconsolate as I had ever seen him as he spoke the words. I had lied to him so many times before in the name of duty and country. Why couldn't I lie to him now?

"Of course I love you," came my choked whisper. "That isn't the point."

He took another step toward me. "Love is always the point. It's the point of everything."

His gaze was so soft as he looked down at me, I thought that I might break. I had been so alone for so long—so selfless that I had ignored my basic need: for somebody, just once, to care for me.

I knew in my heart that he loved me. He needn't have said it out loud. I knew that he wanted—and intended—to care for me.

"I have always wanted you, Zain. You don't know how sorely I regret every day that I let you believe otherwise. I'm begging you now. Please give us a chance. You've seen the fate of lovelorn men with powers run amok. I shudder to think of what might become of me were I to commit crimes of passion in the name of love.

"You can break up with me if I snore too loudly or cook too badly or mess up the wine we grow."

"The wine we grow?" I repeated.

He motioned past me. "I couldn't help but notice your vineyards out back."

"You would want to live here?"

Xabi finally touched me, taking my hand in one of his and bringing the other to smooth over my hair and down my neck. His eyes were as clear and beautiful as ever.

"I want to live wherever you are. And, thanks to my unfathomable privilege, the logistics will work out. Wherever you're working, wherever I'm working, the Queen has delivered a biplane and a jet, just for us."

"Queen Maialen?" I nearly squawked, as if there were any other.

"The most prescient of us all," he murmured. "She saw this coming all along. Gave me a good scolding, too, for not having moved sooner. We will be quite a powerful couple, you know, me as a direct power and you as a sixteenth…"

"Yes," I whispered from nowhere, though he hadn't posed the question in quite some time.

"Yes?" His eyes searched mine with cautious hope.

He let out a tiny sob I didn't know he had been holding and leaned forward until our foreheads touched.

The next thing I knew, our arms were around one another's backs and we were fused together at the waist and I was poised to be on the receiving end of a sweet and hungry kiss. My stomach chose that very instant to let out a ferocious growl.

I groaned in response. Xabi chuckled and jutted his chin down at the forgotten takeout bag.

"What's for dinner, love?" he asked, kissing me on my chin instead and gazing down at me in humor.

"Oysters and mignonette."

He leaned in again, looking as if he intended to kiss me anyway.

"Perfect. An aphrodisiac."

∼

I HOPED you loved Xabier and Zain's story! I truly loved writing it. I used to live in the Basque Country and I really loved thinking about a fictional place in that region of the world. I hope to write more books for this series, but that hasn't happened as yet. Check out our series page for more Royal Powers fun. And if you like my writing, check out *Adam Bomb*, another gay contemporary romance!

AND AFTER YOU pick up *Adam Bomb*, don't forget to subscribe to the Kenzie Blades newsletter. I give away a LOT of freebies and we have a lot of fun.

ABOUT THE
AUTHOR

Kenzie Blades is a queer author of romantic LGBTQIA+ fiction and is the alter ego of a multi-award winning author who writes other fiction under a different name.

Kenzie lives in San Francisco and enjoys lots of things that start with the letter B, like bacon, bourbon and books. Boys, too. Because—come on—they're beautiful.

ACKNOWLEDGEMENTS

Huge, enormous thanks to Chris Cox for organizing this fun collection. I kind of want to live in Abarra now. Don't you? Also, a special thanks to EJ Russell for having the kind of brain who can keep a universe like this organized. I'll also shout-out to Renae Kaye, Lynn Lorenz, Sara York and Jackie North, all of who added super-fun elements to the universe and who have been fun to hang out with online. I can't wait to write more for this series. Abarra has been a great place to escape to during troubled times.

Along those lines, I have to acknowledge my extended team, who are the people who keep me motivated every day and who are with me through the vicissitudes of writing (and life). Rebecca Kimmel of the Writing Refinery fixes all of my copy and is a stellar sort of all-around person. Edward Giordano is my assistant and keeps me organized in all sorts of ways. R.L. Merrill, my Tuesday night Chez Shannon crew, and my plotting ladies, Eva Moore and Wendy Goodman. Thank you, thank you, and thank you.

EXPLORE MORE
ROYAL POWERS

#1 Duking it Out by E.J. Russell

#2 The Hero and the Hidden Royal by Renae Kaye

#3 The Marquis of Secret Doors by Lynn Lorenz

#4 The Lost Prince by Sara York

#5 Pauper Prince Saves the Posh Pullet by Chris Cox

#6 The Duke of Hand to Hart by Jackie North

#7 The Prince and the Pencil Pusher by Kenzie Blades

#8 Our Gay Au Pair by Chris Cox

Made in the USA
Columbia, SC
19 August 2024